TWENTIETH CENTURY VIEWS

The aim of this series is to present the best in contemporary critical opinion on major authors, providing a twentieth century perspective on their changing status in an era of profound revaluation.

Maynard Mack, *Series Editor*
Yale University

OSCAR WILDE

OSCAR WILDE

A COLLECTION OF CRITICAL ESSAYS

Edited by
Richard Ellmann

Prentice-Hall, Inc. *Englewood Cliffs, N.J.*

A SPECTRUM BOOK

Current printing (last number):

10   9   8   7   6   5   4   3   2   1

PRENTICE-HALL INTERNATIONAL, INC. (*London*)
PRENTICE-HALL OF AUSTRALIA, PTY. LTD. (*Sydney*)
PRENTICE-HALL OF CANADA, LTD. (*Toronto*)
PRENTICE-HALL OF INDIA PRIVATE LIMITED (*New Delhi*)
PRENTICE-HALL OF JAPAN, INC. (*Tokyo*)

Contents

OSCAR WILDE

Introduction

by Richard Ellmann

From 1888 to 1895 literary England was put out of countenance by an Irishman who avowed he was a socialist, hinted he was a homosexual, and patently was an antagonist of organized morals and religion. He declined, in the most public and ceremonious manner, to live within his income, behave modestly, work hard, respect his elders, or in general to recognize Reality, Nature, Art, Politics, or History in their traditional attire. Except that his gold-tipped cigarettes contained only tobacco, he was bent on a subversion of propriety and sobriety just as disestablishmentarian as anything out of San Francisco, and much more lavishly got up. Then, at the very moment when he was writing his best, when *The Importance of Being Earnest* was playing to packed houses, he was convicted of what the law picturesquely calls sodomy, and sentenced to two years at hard labor. Following his release he went to the continent and wrote "The Ballad of Reading Gaol," after publishing which, slighted by old acquaintances, he continued to misbehave. In 1900 he died—as he said he had lived—beyond his means.

His contemporaries, recovering from the snubs they had administered to him in person, now entertained him gladly in their memoirs, and many a dull chronicle—as, in life, many a dull table—was posthumously enlivened by this *boulevardier*. His position as a symbolic figure is as engrossing as his works. Among the writers of his time who do not, like Henry James, transcend it altogether, Wilde is the most conspicuous survivor. This position is assured on the continent as well: students of the language find out at once the pungency of his English, which comes, whether he is writing discursively or dramatically, from its being alive with concession and rejection. Rhythms of an older generation's reassuring platitudes and proverbial certainties are undercut by those of intransigent

1

youth. Yet the utmost joviality is marshaled to represent the generations at loggerheads. Wilde abjured the ponderousness which or-
dinarily accompanies social protest. It did not suit him, and innu-
endo could strike deeper.

Some of Wilde's attributes emerge from the responses he provoked in W. B. Yeats and André Gide, who came to know him during his heyday. Yeats wrote, "My first meeting with Oscar Wilde
was an astonishment." At this encounter, which took place in 1888,
he was astonished primarily by the perfect form of Wilde's most
casual utterances, but he was soon impressed as well by the series
of esthetic assumptions and propositions which Wilde had been
shaping and refining for ten years. These were not necessarily original: some came from Flaubert, Gautier, and the French symbolists.
But when Wilde took them over they no longer seemed—as they did
when transmitted by Arthur Symons or George Moore—exotic. Nor
did they seem rarefied or specialized: Wilde gave them universal
relevance by making them objectionable. At the moment when
Yeats felt compelled to build his own esthetic, it was propitious to
hear Wilde argue "the truth of masks," and insist that men direct
their conduct not by moral tenets but by images furnished through
art, that what we behold in nature, as what we make of ourselves,
can be imaginatively determined. Yeats found Wilde personally to
be a man of action, giving himself to the demands of the moment,
eager to shine before the real world whether that was the audience
at the theatre or the dinner table. As a result the theories were not
fully explored, but they prompted Yeats to more elaborate theories.
In the same way he recast Wilde's *Salome* as *The King of the Great
Clock Tower,* and, with an arrogance which Wilde would have approved, reduced "The Ballad of Reading Gaol" to half its original
length before including it in *The Oxford Book of Modern Verse.*

Gide's assimilation of Wilde was less serene. Reared in strict
Protestantism, his lipline—as Wilde complained—straight instead
of curved, Gide needed to be set free. Wilde began to unleash him
in 1891 and completed the process in 1895. The two men first met,
it appears, on November 27, 1891; in a letter the next day to Paul
Valéry, Gide spoke of "the esthete Oscar Wilde," a characterization
which might seem pejorative if he did not immediately subjoin,
"*ô admirable, admirable celui-là.*" They began to meet every day,

with and without other people, and for hours on end. In some agita-
tion Gide notified Valéry on December 4, "Wilde piously devotes
himself to killing whatever soul I have left, because he says that to
know an essence you must do away with it; he wants me to regret
my soul. The effort required to destroy a thing takes its measure.
Things become known by being missed." Perhaps a little to the
relief of Gide, the pagan Mephistopheles left Paris in mid-Decem-
ber. On Christmas eve Gide summed up, for Valéry, his new state of
mind, "Since Wilde I scarcely exist." Some natural anxiety over the
change is apparent in his journal, where the entry on New Year's
Day concludes, "Wilde, I believe, did me nothing but harm. I had
more varied emotions, but had forgotten how to bring them into
order." Forced to reconstitute himself, he was not altogether grati-
fied at the prospect.

Wilde's writings of 1891—*The Picture of Dorian Gray, Intentions, The Soul of Man under Socialism*—indicate with what pro-
nouncements he set about breaking down Gide's scrupulosity. A
life might be fabricated like a work of art, he urged, and the idea
appears sometime later, no longer as Wilde's, in Gide's *Journal*.
Religion, Gide's or another's, had no part in this process. For Wilde,
as for Blake, morality was nothing but the flagging of an energy.
The artist's duty, according to Wilde, was to give free play to sensations and temptations, so as to experience more of them and escape
submission to any single one. What seems surrender is thereby
made a victory, since the engaged being is enabled to pass on. In
this context or one like it, Wilde must have urged Gide to destroy
his soul in order to comprehend it. He probably conveyed to Gide
also his theory of the external drama in which we participate with
society. Since the established social structure confines the individual,
the artist must of necessity ally himself with the criminal classes.
"What is termed Sin," he wrote in *The Soul of Man under Socialism,* "is an essential element in progress." He praised, in *Intentions,*
the forger and writer Wainwright, as today he would have praised
Genet, for having—by criminal activity—improved his style. Gide,
shaken, revolted, yet fascinated, remarked later that Wilde had
wished him to "authorize evil." The authorization of evil supplies
much of the subject of *The Immoralist* in 1902, as of *The Counter-
feiters* (1926). Some of Wilde's effect is probably registered in the

Pan-like figure Menalcas, endowed by Gide with Wilde's girth, who appears in both *The Immoralist* and *Fruits of the Earth* (1897).

Wilde's effect on Gide reached its apogee when in 1895 they met fortuitously in Algeria. On that occasion he encouraged his friend (who didn't need much encouragement, but was glad to have some) to spend the night with a young flute player. Gide said that the incident established his homosexual direction, until then inchoate. He did not receive the favor ungrudgingly, for when Wilde came to live in France following his release from prison, Gide visited him once and thereafter generally managed to be out of the vicinity. Gide's essays about Wilde written after the latter's death in 1900 insist, almost too much, upon Wilde's brilliance as a conversationalist and disparage him as a writer. Gide thereby achieves a supremacy not attained during their early acquaintance by depicting Wilde as talking away a talent which Gide could husband in books. Wilde's soft vice likewise becomes Gide's solid, affirmable virtue, to be didactically justified (instead of merely practiced) in his book on homosexuality, *Corydon*. Gide's tendency to belittle Wilde as a writer was so noticeable that Marcel Proust, himself no great admirer of Wilde, urged Gide to desist, and had some effect. Gide felt at fault, and knew that he wished to feel he had transcended this powerful influence upon his youth when in fact, like Yeats, he had also incorporated it.

Gide's susceptibility to Wilde's anti-doctrine makes its potency more apparent. In aiding Gide to acknowledge propensities as yet almost undeveloped, Wilde was glad to confuse (in the way that Walter Pater did and then backed away from doing) instruction with seduction. He wished to represent the "new Hellenism" as arrestingly as he could. There is no evidence that Wilde corrupted anyone (Gide was scarcely an innocent), but his reputation for doing so grew with rumor, and was enhanced by his revamping of the Faust legend in *Dorian Gray*. Seeking after an effect, he did not mind if people thought the effect insidious. Sometimes even people who knew him well fell into predictable tones of reproof. Lionel Johnson, for example, who had admired *Dorian Gray* so much that he testified to his admiration in Latin, soon after veered and addressed a sonnet, in a less dorian mode, "To the Destroyer of a Soul." The soul was presumably that of Lord Alfred Douglas, whom

Johnson had introduced to Wilde. On the other hand, Johnson made a final tergiversation, according to Yeats, and became at last Wilde's fanatical defender. Among many reactions, none was tepid.

The name of Lord Alfred Douglas belongs to the history of love rather than of literature, although he wrote many poems and played poet. Douglas was twenty-one when he and Wilde met; he was already being blackmailed by a "renter" (male prostitute) from whose demands he asked Wilde to save him. For four years he gloried in being Wilde's "minion" and in enticing his lover into greater and greater demonstrations of protection. Wilde seems to have needed some lasting attachment to balance his philandering, but Bosie proved to be more than an attachment—a malady, rather. It was a case, as W. H. Auden takes note, of the Overloved (Wilde) meeting the Underloved. Douglas needed to make Wilde wretched so as to exhibit power over him, and Wilde's vanity found a subtle outlet in seeing how much of Bosie's tyranny he could endure.

Life with Bosie was a continuous quarrel which did not stop after Wilde's death, because the long letter to Douglas from prison, known as *De Profundis,* was released by Wilde's friend Robert Ross in successively fuller versions, each of which added a few more strictures on Bosie's conduct. Douglas felt obliged to write answer after answer, sometimes in poems or letters but also in several books. After exalting he excoriated, then largely forgave, his dead friend. The best of his bad poems celebrated Wilde in 1901, the most contemptible was that written in 1924, when Douglas, a devotee of libel suits, was himself jailed for criminal libel of Winston Churchill. In Wormwood Scrubs prison he wrote a sonnet sequence entitled *In Excelsis*—a riposte to *De Profundis*—and blamed Wilde in it for having perverted both himself and England. He later withdrew the allegation but reprinted the poem.

Until his conviction Wilde liked to picture himself as the type of artist-criminal, although it was not certain that any of his acts might qualify, in another age, as crimes. But afterwards he saw himself in the nobler role of sufferer, of scapegoat instead of scapegrace. His thoughts revolved increasingly around Christ, whom in *De Profundis* he called the supreme artist because of his recognition and forgiveness of all aberrant behavior. This spirit of forgiveness animates "The Ballad of Reading Gaol," where the malefactor is identified with the other prisoners and then with all humanity. Wilde avoided putting himself forward bluntly as society's victim, but his early death hallowed his life for others who took the hints he had so prodigally broadcast.

He became, then, for many an embodiment of the Christlike artist. James Joyce chose to regard Wilde as such a figure when he wrote about *Salome* for a Triestine newspaper. Having been victimized himself by an unofficial English censorship, he was ready to see Wilde as his forerunner in the battle with imperial hypocrisy, Christ against Caesar. In a later generation Hart Crane, while still very young, wrote the poem "C 33" (Wilde's number in prison), and out of homosexual sympathy conferred on Wilde, as on all subsequent objects of his affection, instant apotheosis. G. Wilson Knight has developed the Christlike aspect of Wilde with more attention to historical detail; he shows that the imagery in Wilde's stories prefigured his fall. Wilde not only implied an analogy but, Knight feels, may be said to have merited it.

Neither Gide nor Yeats exalted Wilde in this way, nor Bernard Shaw, also acquainted with him. Shaw thought Wilde never played the role of martyr with conviction, and chalked this up to his friend's credit. Gide saw Wilde in his last years as broken rather than self-vindicated or triumphant. For Yeats the analogue was not Christ but Masoch: Wilde, he said, was one of the men and women "who love those who rob or beat them, as though the soul were intoxicated by its discovery of human nature, or found even a secret delight in the shattering of the image of its desire. It is as though it cried, 'I would be possessed by' or 'I would possess that which is human. What do I care if it is good or bad?' There is no 'disillusionment,' for they have found that which they have sought, but that which they have sought and found is a fragment."

The most recent criticism of Wilde has generally, except in the case of Wilson Knight, refused to mythologize him as either noble criminal or Christ. Brendan Behan's poem, "Oscar Wilde," salutes him for both sinning and repenting, for living it up in both modes. A well-known poem of John Betjeman plays on the stereotypes of Wilde, the policemen, and the manager of the Cadogan Hotel where Wilde's arrest took place, and makes them all stagey and pretentious. There is no tragedy, only solemn farce. George Woodcock finds in him a surprisingly steady adherence to philosophic, and secular, anarchism. The most effective demythologizing of Wilde has been that of W. H. Auden, who entitled one of his essays on him, "Saint Oscar the Homintern Martyr." Auden finds Wilde on Christ or redemption through suffering to be just as "childish and boring" as Gide on the same subjects. He presents him instead as a fallible, brilliant, marvelous *performer* who, egged on by the horrible Bosie, lost relation to the audience he so much needed.

A number of critics have tried to estimate Wilde's works apart from the legends that surround their author. Edouard Roditi shows that *Dorian Gray,* however woodenly it follows in the tradition of the Gothic romance and of the novel about dandies, carries within it intimations of a more profound myth "beyond good and evil." There is general agreement that Wilde's critical dialogues and the plays, especially *The Importance of Being Earnest* and *Lady Windermere's Fan,* are his best work. (*Salome,* improved into an opera by Strauss, also appears to keep some of the allurement that Wilde too generously lavished upon it.) His plays can still be seen fairly frequently in theatres in Paris or Moscow as well as in London or parts of the United States. His anti-moralism and floridity have lately found a distinct vogue as "camp."

The Importance of Being Earnest, which St. John Hankin as a fellow playwright calls "artistically the most serious work that Wilde produced for the theatre," has aroused most controversy. Bernard Shaw, who liked Wilde's earlier plays, thought that this last one showed a decline because of its heartlessness, especially with regard to women. Mary McCarthy doesn't mind the heartlessness, and rather soberly welcomes depravity as the hero—surely an overstatement. Her objection is rather to the jokes, which she thinks are overworked. The play is almost saved for her by Lady Bracknell, whom she finds to be a Queen-Victoria figure; but this regal characterization seems to deny Lady Bracknell any consciousness of her own wit. Eric Bentley considers the play to be an attack upon a series of moral foibles, the more piercing because it pretends not to pierce at all. Auden, less concerned with high purpose, regards the play as the only pure verbal opera in English. Social concerns are words in a game, with nothing more intended, and Wilde's feat is in keeping them from being anything else. By a paradox that would have pleased Wilde, the play has become a Victorian period-piece, although its chief effect is to reduce Victorian pieties to the level of amiable idiocies.

As public tolerance of homosexuality has increased, Wilde's reputation has stood firm, indicating that it never depended upon his being a sublime, or not sublime, pariah. In the age of Genet and Albee his bonhomie has a new attractiveness. But his persistence comes from a further quality. Jorge Luis Borges, whose own work has much affinity with Wilde's and often reads like a late offshoot of estheticism, points out how often Wilde, besides being witty, is *right*. Thomas Mann, although he likes Nietzsche better, has to admit that Wilde and Nietzsche greatly resemble each other. As Mann says, the first great challenge to the existing order was the esthetic revolt. That order still exists, and Wilde's revolt against it continues to make sense.

My First Meeting with Oscar Wilde

by *William Butler Yeats*

My first meeting with Oscar Wilde was an astonishment. I
never before heard a man talking with perfect sentences, as if he had
written them all overnight with labour and yet all spontaneous.
There was present that night at Henley's, by right of propinquity
or of accident, a man full of the secret spite of dullness, who interrupted from time to time, and always to check or disorder thought;
and I noticed with what mastery he was foiled and thrown. I noticed, too, that the impression of artificiality that I think all Wilde's
listeners have recorded came from the perfect rounding of the sentences and from the deliberation that made it possible. That very
impression helped him, as the effect of metre, or of the antithetical
prose of the seventeenth century, which is itself a true metre, helped
its writers, for he could pass without incongruity from some unfore-
seen, swift stroke of wit to elaborate reverie. I heard him say a few
nights later: "Give me *The Winter's Tale*, 'Daffodils that come before the swallow dare' but not *King Lear*. What is *King Lear* but
poor life staggering in the fog?" and the slow, carefully modulated
cadence sounded natural to my ears. That first night he praised
Walter Pater's *Studies in the History of the Renaissance:* "It is my
golden book; I never travel anywhere without it; but it is the very
flower of decadence: the last trumpet should have sounded the moment it was written." "But," said the dull man, "would you not
have given us time to read it?" "Oh no," was the retort, "there would
have been plenty of time afterwards—in either world." I think he

"My First Meeting with Oscar Wilde" (Editor's title). From *The Trembling
of the Veil*, in *Autobiography* by William Butler Yeats (New York and London:
The Macmillan Company, 1916), pp. 79–85. Copyright 1916, 1936 by The Macmillan Company; renewed 1944 by Bertha Georgie Yeats. Reprinted by permission of The Macmillan Company, Macmillan & Co., Ltd., and Mr. M. B. Yeats.

seemed to us, baffled as we were by youth, or by infirmity, a triumphant figure, and to some of us a figure from another age, an
audacious Italian fifteenth-century figure. A few weeks before I had
heard one of my father's friends, an official in a publishing firm
that had employed both Wilde and Henley as editors, blaming
Henley who was "no use except under control" and praising Wilde,
"so indolent but such a genius"; and now the firm became the topic
of our talk. "How often do you go to the office?" said Henley. "I
used to go three times a week," said Wilde, "for an hour a day but
I have since struck off one of the days." "My God," said Henley, "I
went five times a week for five hours a day and when I wanted to
strike off a day they had a special committee meeting." "Further-
more," was Wilde's answer, "I never answered their letters. I have
known men come to London full of bright prospects and seen them
complete wrecks in a few months through a habit of answering letters." He too knew how to keep our elders in their place, and his
method was plainly the more successful, for Henley had been dismissed. "No he is not an aesthete," Henley commented later, being
somewhat embarrassed by Wilde's pre-Raphaelite entanglement;
"one soon finds that he is a scholar and a gentleman." And when I
dined with Wilde a few days afterwards he began at once, "I had
to strain every nerve to equal that man at all"; and I was too loyal
to speak my thought: "You and not he said all the brilliant things."
He like the rest of us had felt the strain of an intensity that seemed
to hold life at the point of drama. He had said on that first meeting,
"The basis of literary friendship is mixing the poisoned bowl"; and
for a few weeks Henley and he became close friends till, the astonishment of their meeting over, diversity of character and ambition
pushed them apart, and, with half the cavern helping, Henley began mixing the poisoned bowl for Wilde. Yet Henley never wholly
lost that first admiration, for after Wilde's downfall he said to me:
"Why did he do it? I told my lads to attack him and yet we might
have fought under his banner."

It became the custom, both at Henley's and at Bedford Park, to
say that R. A. M. Stevenson, who frequented both circles, was the
better talker. Wilde had been trussed up like a turkey by under-

graduates, dragged up and down a hill, his champagne emptied into the ice tub, hooted in the streets of various towns, and I think stoned, and no newspaper named him but in scorn; his manner had hardened to meet opposition and at times he allowed one to see an unpardonable insolence. His charm was acquired and systematised, a mask which he wore only when it pleased him, while the charm of Stevenson belonged to him like the colour of his hair. If Stevenson's talk became monologue we did not know it, because our one object was to show by our attention that he need never leave off. If thought failed him we would not combat what he had said, or start some new theme, but would encourage him with a question; and one felt that it had been always so from childhood up. His mind was full of fantasy for fantasy's sake and he gave us good entertainment in monologue as his cousin Robert Louis in poem or story. He was always "supposing"; "Suppose you had two millions what would you do with it?" and "Suppose you were in Spain and in love how would you propose?" I recall him one afternoon at our house at Bedford Park, surrounded by my brother and sisters and a little group of my father's friends, describing proposals in a half dozen countries. There your father did it, dressed in such and such a way with such and such words, and there a friend must wait for the lady outside the chapel door, sprinkle her with holy water and say, "My friend Jones is dying for love of you." But when it was over those quaint descriptions, so full of laughter and sympathy, faded or remained in the memory as something alien from one's own life, like a dance I once saw in a great house, where beautifully dressed children wound a long ribbon in and out as they danced. I was not of Stevenson's party mainly I think because he had written a book in praise of Velasquez, praise at that time universal wherever pre-Raphaelism was accurst, and to my mind, that had to pick its symbols where its ignorance permitted, Velasquez seemed the first bored celebrant of boredom. I was convinced from some obscure meditation that Stevenson's conversational method had joined him to my elders and to the indifferent world, as though it were right for old men, and unambitious men and all women, to be content with charm and humour. It was the prerogative of youth to take sides and when Wilde said: "Mr. Bernard Shaw has no enemies but is in-

tensely disliked by all his friends," I knew it to be a phrase I should
never forget, and felt revenged upon a notorious hater of romance,
whose generosity and courage I could not fathom.

   I saw a good deal of Wilde at that time—was it 1887 or 1888?—
I have no way of fixing the date except that I had published my
first book *The Wanderings of Usheen* and that Wilde had not yet
published his *Decay of Lying*. He had, before our first meeting, reviewed my book and despite its vagueness of intention, and the
inexactness of its speech, praised without qualification; and what
was worth more than any review he had talked about it; and now
he asked me to eat my Christmas dinner with him believing, I imagine, that I was alone in London. He had just renounced his vel-
veteen, and even those cuffs turned backward over the sleeves, and
had begun to dress very carefully in the fashion of the moment. He
lived in a little house at Chelsea that the architect Godwin had
decorated with an elegance that owed something to Whistler. There
was nothing mediæval, nor pre-Raphaelite, no cupboard door with
figures upon flat gold, no peacock-blue, no dark background. I remember vaguely a white drawing-room with Whistler etchings, "let
in" to white panels, and a dining-room all white, chairs, walls, man-
telpiece, carpet, except for a diamond-shaped piece of red cloth in
the middle of the table under a terra-cotta statuette, and I think a
red-shaded lamp hanging from the ceiling to a little above the statuette. It was perhaps too perfect in its unity, his past of a few years
before had gone too completely, and I remember thinking that the
perfect harmony of his life there, with his beautiful wife and his
two young children, suggested some deliberate artistic composition.
   He commended and dispraised himself during dinner by attribut-
ing characteristics like his own to his country: "We Irish are too
poetical to be poets; we are a nation of brilliant failures, but we are
the greatest talkers since the Greeks." When dinner was over he
read me from the proofs of the *Decay of Lying* and when he came to
the sentence: "Schopenhauer has analysed the pessimism that char-
acterises modern thought, but Hamlet invented it. The world has
become sad because a puppet was once melancholy," I said, "Why
do you change 'sad' to 'melancholy'?" He replied that he wanted a
full sound at the close of his sentence, and I thought it no excuse

and an example of the vague impressiveness that spoilt his writing
for me. Only when he spoke, or when his writing was the mirror of
his speech, or in some simple fairy tale, had he words exact enough
to hold a subtle ear. He alarmed me, though not as Henley did, for
I never left his house thinking myself fool or dunce. He flattered the
intellect of every man he liked; he made me tell him long Irish
stories and compared my art of story-telling to Homer's; and once
when he had described himself as writing in the census paper "age
19, profession genius, infirmity talent" the other guest, a young
journalist fresh from Oxford or Cambridge, said, "What should I
have written?" and was told that it should have been "profession
talent, infirmity genius." When, however, I called, wearing shoes a
little too yellow—unblackened leather had just become fashionable
—I realised their extravagance when I saw his eyes fixed upon
them; and another day Wilde asked me to tell his little boy a fairy
story, and I had but got as far as "Once upon a time there was a
giant" when the little boy screamed and ran out of the room. Wilde
looked grave and I was plunged into the shame of clumsiness that
afflicts the young. And when I asked for some literary gossip for
some provincial newspaper, that paid me a few shillings a month, I
was told that writing literary gossip was no job for a gentleman.

Though to be compared to Homer passed the time pleasantly, I
had not been greatly perturbed had he stopped me with: "Is it a
long story?" as Henley would certainly have done. I was abashed
before him as wit and man of the world alone. I remember that he
deprecated the very general belief in his success or his efficiency, and
I think with sincerity. One form of success had gone: he was no
more the lion of the season and he had not discovered his gift for
writing comedy, yet I think I knew him at the happiest moment of
his life. No scandal had touched his name, his fame as a talker was
growing among his equals, and he seemed to live in the enjoyment
of his own spontaneity. One day he began: "I have been inventing
a Christian heresy," and he told a detailed story, in the style of some
early father, of how Christ recovered after the Crucifixion, and es-
caping from the tomb, lived on for many years, the one man upon
earth who knew the falsehood of Christianity. Once St. Paul visited
his town and he alone in the carpenters' quarter did not go to hear
him preach. Henceforth the other carpenters noticed that, for some

unknown reason, he kept his hands covered. A few days afterwards I found Wilde with smock frocks in various colours spread out upon the floor in front of him, while a missionary explained that he did not object to the heathen going naked upon weekdays, but insisted upon clothes in church. He had brought the smock frocks in a cab that the only art-critic whose fame had reached Central Africa might select a colour; so Wilde sat there weighing all with a conscious ecclesiastic solemnity.

Of late years I have often explained Wilde to myself by his family history. His father was a friend or acquaintance of my father's father and among my family traditions there is an old Dublin riddle: "Why are Sir William Wilde's nails so black?" Answer, "Because he has scratched himself." And there is an old story still current in Dublin of Lady Wilde saying to a servant, "Why do you put the plates on the coal-scuttle? What are the chairs meant for?" They were famous people and there are many like stories; and even a horrible folk story, the invention of some Connaught peasant, that tells how Sir William Wilde took out the eyes of some men, who had come to consult him as an oculist, and laid them upon a plate, intending to replace them in a moment, and how the eyes were eaten by a cat. As a certain friend of mine, who has made a prolonged study of the nature of cats, said when he first heard the tale, "Cats love eyes." The Wilde family was clearly of the sort that fed the imagination of Charles Lever, dirty, untidy, daring, and what Charles Lever, who loved more normal activities, might not have valued so highly, very imaginative and learned. Lady Wilde, who when I knew her received her friends with blinds drawn and shutters closed that none might see her withered face, longed always perhaps, though certainly amid much self-mockery, for some impossible splendour of character and circumstance. She lived near her son in level Chelsea, but I have heard her say, "I want to live on some high place, Primrose Hill or Highgate, because I was an eagle in my youth." I think her son lived with no self-mockery at all, an imaginary life; perpetually performed a play which was in all things the opposite of all that he had known in childhood and early youth; never put off completely his wonder at opening his eyes every morning on his own beautiful house, and in remembering that he had dined yesterday with a duchess, and that he delighted in Flaubert and Pater, read Homer in the original and not as a schoolmaster reads him for the grammar. I think, too, that because of all that half-civilised blood in his veins he could not endure the sedentary toil of creative art and so remained a man of action, exaggerating, for the sake of immediate effect, every trick learned from his masters, turning their easel painting into painted scenes. He was a parvenu, but a parvenu whose whole bearing proved that if he did dedicate every story in *The House of Pomegranates* to a lady of title, it was but to show that he was Jack and the social ladder his pantomime beanstalk. "Did you ever hear him say 'Marquess of Dimmesdale'?" a friend of his once asked me. "He does not say 'the Duke of York' with any pleasure."

He told me once that he had been offered a safe seat in Parliament and, had he accepted, he might have had a career like that of Beaconsfield, whose early style resembles his, being meant for crowds, for excitement, for hurried decisions, for immediate triumphs. Such men get their sincerity, if at all, from the contact of events; the dinner table was Wilde's event and made him the greatest talker of his time, and his plays and dialogues have what merit they possess from being now an imitation, now a record, of his talk. Even in those days I would often defend him by saying that his very admiration for his predecessors in poetry, for Browning, for Swinburne and Rossetti, in their first vogue while he was a very young man, made any success seem impossible that could satisfy his immense ambition; never but once before had the artist seemed so great, never had the work of art seemed so difficult. I would then compare him with Benvenuto Cellini who, coming after Michael Angelo, found nothing left to do so satisfactory as to turn bravo and quarrel with the man who broke Michael Angelo's nose.

The Catastrophe

by *William Butler Yeats*

Shaw and Wilde, had no catastrophe come, would have long divided the stage between them, though they were most unlike— for Wilde believed himself to value nothing but words in their emotional associations, and he had turned his style to a parade as though it were his show, and he Lord Mayor.

I was at Sligo again and I saw the announcement of his action against Lord Queensbury, when starting from my uncle's home to walk to Knocknarea to dine with Cochrane of the Glen, as he was called, to distinguish him from others of that name, an able old man. He had a relation, a poor mad girl, who shared our meals, and at whom I shuddered. She would take a flower from the vase in front of her and push it along the tablecloth towards any male guest who sat near. The old man himself had strange opinions, born not from any mental eccentricity, but from the solitude of his life; and a freedom from all prejudices that were not of his own discovery. "The world is getting more manly," he would say, "it has begun to drink port again," or "Ireland is going to become prosperous. Divorced couples now choose Ireland for a retreat, just as before Scotland became prosperous they began to go there. There are a divorced wife and her lover living at the other side of the mountain." I remember that I spoke that night of Wilde's kindness to myself, said I did not believe him guilty, quoted the psychologist Bain, who has attributed to every sensualist "a voluminous tenderness," and described Wilde's hard brilliance, his dominating self-

"The Catastrophe" (Editor's title). From "The Tragic Generation," in *Autobiography* by William Butler Yeats (New York and London: The Macmillan Company, 1916), pp. 170–74. Copyright 1916, 1936 by The Macmillan Company; renewed 1944 by Bertha Georgie Yeats. Reprinted by permission of The Macmillan Company, Macmillan & Co., Ltd., and Mr. M. B. Yeats.

possession. I considered him essentially a man of action, that he was a writer by perversity and accident, and would have been more important as soldier or politician; and I was certain that, guilty or not guilty, he would prove himself a man. I was probably excited, and did most of the talking, for if Cochrane had talked, I would have remembered an amusing sentence or two; but he was certainly sympathetic. A couple of days later I received a letter from Lionel Johnson, denouncing Wilde with great bitterness. He had "a cold scientific intellect"; he got a "sense of triumph and power, at every dinner-table he dominated, from the knowledge that he was guilty of that sin which, more than any other possible to man, would turn all those people against him if they but knew." He wrote in the mood of his poem, *To the Destroyer of a Soul,* addressed to Wilde, as I have always believed, though I know nothing of the circumstance that made him write it.

I might have known that Wilde's fantasy had taken some tragic turn, and that he was meditating upon possible disaster, but one took all his words for play—had he not called insincerity "a mere multiplication of the personality" or some such words? I had met a man who had found him in a barber's shop in Venice, and heard him explain, "I am having my hair curled that I may resemble Nero"; and when, as editor of an Irish anthology, I had asked leave to quote "Tread gently, she is near under the snow," he had written that I might do so if I pleased, but his most characteristic poem was that sonnet with the lines

> Lo! with a little rod
> I did but touch the honey of romance—
> And must I lose a soul's inheritance.

When in London for my play I had asked news from an actor who had seen him constantly. "He is in deep melancholy," was the answer. "He says that he tries to sleep away as much of life as possible, only leaving his bed at two or three in the afternoon, and spending the rest of the day at the Café Royal. He has written what he calls the best short story in the world, and will have it that he repeats to himself on getting out of bed and before every meal, 'Christ came from a white plain to a purple city, and as he passed through the first street, he heard voices overhead, and saw a young man lying drunk upon a window-sill, "Why do you waste your soul in drunkenness?" He said. "Lord, I was a leper and you healed me, what else can I do?" A little further through the town he saw a young man following a harlot, and said, "Why do you dissolve your soul in debauchery?" and the young man answered, "Lord, I was blind, and You healed me, what else can I do?" At last in the middle of the city He saw an old man crouching, weeping upon the ground, and when He asked why he wept, the old man answered, "Lord, I was dead and You raised me into life, what else can I do but weep?' "

Wilde published that story a little later, but spoiled it with the verbal decoration of his epoch, and I have to repeat it to myself as I first heard it, before I can see its terrible beauty. I no more doubt its sincerity than I doubt that his parade of gloom, all that late rising, and sleeping away his life, that elaborate playing with tragedy, was an attempt to escape from an emotion by its exaggeration. He had three successful plays running at once; he had been almost poor, and now, his head full of Flaubert, found himself with ten thousand a year:—"Lord, I was dead, and You raised me into life, what else can I do but weep." A comedian, he was in the hands of those dramatists who understand nothing but tragedy.

A few days after the first production of my *Land of Heart's Desire,* I had my last conversation with him. He had come into the theatre as the curtain fell upon my play, and I knew that it was to ask my pardon that he overwhelmed me with compliments; and yet I wonder if he would have chosen those precise compliments, or spoken so extravagantly, but for the turn his thoughts had taken: "Your story in *The National Observer,* 'The Crucifixion of the Outcast,' is sublime, wonderful, wonderful."

Some business or other brought me to London once more and I asked various Irish writers for letters of sympathy, and I was refused by none but Edward Dowden, who gave me what I considered an irrelevant excuse—his dislike for everything that Wilde had written. I heard that Wilde was at his mother's house in Oakley Street, and I called there, but the Irish servant said, her face drawn and tragic as in the presence of death, that he was not there, but that I could see his brother. Willie Wilde received me with, "Who are you; what do you want?" but became all friendship when I told him that I had brought letters of sympathy. He took the bundle of letters in his hand, but said, "Do these letters urge him to run away? Every friend he has is urging him to, but we have made up our minds that he must stay and take his chance." "No," I said, "I certainly do not think that he should run away, nor do those letters advise it." "Letters from Ireland," he said. "Thank you, thank you. He will be glad to get those letters, but I would keep them from him if they advised him to run away." Then he threw himself back in his chair and began to talk with incoherent emotion, and in phrases that echoed now and again his brother's style at its worst; there were tears in his eyes, and he was, I think, slightly intoxicated. "He could escape, oh, yes, he could escape—there is a yacht in the Thames, and five thousand pounds to pay his bail—well not exactly in the Thames, but there is a yacht—oh, yes, he could escape, even if I had to inflate a balloon in the back-yard with my own hand, but he has resolved to stay, to face it out, to stand the music like Christ. You must have heard—it is not necessary to go into detail —that he and I have not been friends; but he came to me like a wounded stag, and I took him in." "After his release"—after he had been bailed out I suppose—"Stewart Headlam engaged a room at an hotel and brought him there under another name, but the manager came up and said, 'Are you Mr. Wilde?' You know what my brother is, you know how he would answer that. He said, 'Yes, I am Oscar Wilde,' and the manager said he must not stay. The same thing happened in hotel after hotel, and at last he made up his mind to come here. It is his vanity that has brought all this disgrace upon him; they swung incense before him." He dwelt upon the rhythm of the words as his brother would have done—"They swung it before his heart." His first emotion at the thought of the letters over, he became more simple, and explained that his brother considered that his crime was not the vice itself, but that he should have brought such misery upon his wife and children, and that he was bound to accept any chance, however slight, to re-establish his position. "If he is acquitted," he said, "he will stay out of England for a few years, and can then gather his friends about him once more—even if he is condemned he will purge his offence—but if he runs away he will lose every friend that he has." I heard later, from whom I forget now, that Lady Wilde had said, "If you stay, even if you go to prison, you will always be my son, it will make no difference to my affection, but if you go, I will never speak to you again." While I was there, some woman who had just seen him— Willie Wilde's wife, I think—came in, and threw herself in a chair, and said in an exhausted voice, "It is all right now, he has made up his mind to go to prison if necessary." Before his release, two years later, his brother and mother were dead, and a little later his wife, struck by paralysis during his imprisonment, I think, was dead, too; and he himself, his constitution ruined by prison life, followed quickly; but I have never doubted, even for an instant, that he made the right decision, and that he owes to that decision half of his renown.

Cultivated London, that before the action against Lord Queensberry had mocked his pose and his affected style, and refused to acknowledge his wit, was now full of his advocates, though I did not meet a single man who considered him innocent. One old enemy of his overtook me in the street and began to praise his audacity, his self-possession. "He has made," he said, "of infamy a new Thermopylæ." I had written in reply to Lionel Johnson's letter that I regretted Wilde's downfall but not that of his imitators, but Johnson had changed with the rest. "Why do you not regret the fall of Wilde's imitators"—I had but tried to share what I thought his opinion—"They were worthless, but should have been left to criticism." Wilde himself was a martyr in his eyes, and when I said that tragedy might give his art a greater depth, he would not even grant a martyr's enemies that poor merit, and thought Wilde would produce, when it was all over, some comedy exactly like the others, writing from an art where events could leave no trace. Everywhere one met writers and artists who praised his wit and eloquence in the witness-box, or repeated some private saying. Willie Redmond told of finding him, to his astonishment, at the conversazione of some theatrical society, standing amid an infuriated crowd, mocking with more than all his old satirical wit the actors and their country. He had said to a well-known painter during one or other of the trials, "My poor brother writes to me that he is defending me all over London; my poor, dear brother, he could compromise a steam engine." His brother, too, had suffered a change, for, if rumour did not wrong him, "the wounded stag" had not been at all graciously received. "Thank God my vices were decent," had been his comment, and refusing to sit at the same table, he had dined at some neighbouring hotel at his brother's expense. His successful brother who had scorned him for a drunken ne'er-do-well was now at his mercy, and besides, he probably shared, until tragedy awoke another self, the rage and contempt that filled the crowds in the street, and all men and women who had an over-abundant normal sexual instinct. "Wilde will never lift his head again," said the art critic, Gleeson White, "for he has against him all men of infamous life." When the verdict was announced the harlots in the street outside danced upon the pavement.

Wilde in Phase 19

by *William Butler Yeats*

PHASE NINETEEN[1]

Will—The Assertive Man.
Mask (from Phase 5). *True*—Conviction. *False*—Domination.
Creative Mind (from Phase 11). *True*—Emotional intellect. *False*—
The Unfaithful.
  Body of Fate (from Phase 25)—Enforced failure of action.
  Examples: Gabriele d'Annunzio (perhaps), Oscar Wilde, Byron, a
certain actress.

This phase is the beginning of the artificial, the abstract, the
fragmentary, and the dramatic. Unity of Being is no longer possible,
for the being is compelled to live in a fragment of itself and to
dramatise that fragment. The *primary tincture* is closing, direct
knowledge of self in relation to action is ceasing to be possible.
The being only completely knows that portion of itself which

"Wilde in Phase 19" (Editor's title). From *A Vision* by William Butler Yeats
(New York: The Macmillan Company, 1938), pp. 147–51. Copyright 1926 by
William Butler Yeats; revision 1937 copyright Bertha Georgie Yeats and The
Macmillan Company and 1952 Bertha Georgie Yeats; renewed 1965 by Bertha
Georgie Yeats and Anne Butler Yeats. Reprinted by permission of The Mac-
millan Company, Macmillan & Co., Ltd., and Mr. M. B. Yeats.

[1] In *A Vision* Yeats analyzes the types of human character in terms of the
phases of the moon. At the dark of the moon (phase 1) is pure objectivity
(which he calls the primary tincture). At the full moon (phase 15) is pure
subjectivity (the antithetical tincture). In phases close to the dark, men wish
to be swallowed up, to become virtually anonymous, while in phases close to
the full they wish to be most plentifully themselves. By placing Wilde in Phase
19, Yeats indicates that his compatriot was falling away from a unified selfhood.
  Other special terms used in this passage are Will and Mask, which may be
roughly translated as Imagination and the Image of what one wishes to become; and Creative Mind and Body of Fate, roughly Intellect and the Environment.

judges fact for the sake of action. When the man lives according to phase, he is now governed by conviction, instead of by a ruling mood, and is effective only in so far as he can find this conviction. His aim is so to use an intellect which turns easily to declamation, emotional emphasis, that it serves conviction in a life where effort, just in so far as its object is passionately desired, comes to nothing. He desires to be strong and stable, but as Unity of Being and self-knowledge are both gone, and it is too soon to grasp at another unity through *primary* mind, he passes from emphasis to emphasis. The strength from conviction, derived from a *Mask* of the first quarter *antithetically* transformed, is not founded upon social duty, though that may seem so to others, but is temperamentally formed to fit some crisis of personal life. His thought is immensely effective and dramatic, arising always from some immediate situation, a situation found or created by himself, and may have great permanent value as the expression of an exciting personality. This thought is always an open attack; or a sudden emphasis, an extravagance, or an impassioned declamation of some general idea, which is a more veiled attack. The *Creative Mind* being derived from Phase 11, he is doomed to attempt the destruction of all that breaks or encumbers personality, but this personality is conceived of as a fragmentary, momentary intensity. The mastery of images, threatened or lost at Phase 18, may, however, be completely recovered, but there is less symbol, more fact. Vitality from dreams has died out, and a vitality from fact has begun which has for its ultimate aim the mastery of the real world. The watercourse after an abrupt fall continues upon a lower level; ice turns to water, or water to vapour: there is a new chemical phase.

When lived out of phase there is a hatred or contempt of others, and instead of seeking conviction for its own sake, the man takes up opinions that he may impose himself upon others. He is tyrannical and capricious, and his intellect is called "The Unfaithful," because, being used for victory alone, it will change its ground in a moment and delight in some new emphasis, not caring whether old or new have consistency. The *Mask* is derived from that phase where perversity begins, where artifice begins, and has its *discord* from Phase 25, the last phase where the artificial is possible; the *Body of Fate* is therefore enforced failure of action, and many at this phase desire action above all things as a means of expression. Whether the man be in or out of phase, there is the desire to escape from Unity of Being or any approximation towards it, for Unity can be but a simulacrum now. And in so far as the soul keeps its memory of that potential Unity there is conscious *antithetical* weakness. He must now dramatise the *Mask* through the *Will* and dreads the Image, deep within, of the old *antithetical tincture* at its strongest, and yet this *Image* may seem infinitely desirable if he could but find the desire. When so torn into two, escape when it comes may be so violent that it brings him under the False *Mask* and the False *Creative Mind.* A certain actress is typical, for she surrounds herself with drawings by Burne-Jones in his latest period, and reveres them as they were holy pictures, while her manners are boisterous, dominating and egotistical. They are faces of silent women, and she is not silent for a moment; yet these faces are not, as I once thought, the True *Mask* but a part of that incoherence the True *Mask* must conceal. Were she to surrender to their influence she would become insincere in her art and exploit an emotion that is no longer hers. I find in Wilde, too, something pretty, feminine, and insincere, derived from his admiration for writers of the 17th and earlier phases, and much that is violent, arbitrary and insolent, derived from his desire to escape.

The *antithetical Mask* comes to men of Phase 17 and Phase 18 as a form of strength, and when they are tempted to dramatise it, the dramatisation is fitful, and brings no conviction of strength, for they dislike emphasis; but now the weakness of the *antithetical* has begun, for though still the stronger it cannot ignore the growing *primary*. It is no longer an absolute monarch, and it permits power to pass to statesman or demagogue, whom, however, it will constantly change.

Here one finds men and women who love those who rob them or beat them, as though the soul were intoxicated by its discovery of human nature, or found even a secret delight in the shattering of the image of its desire. It is as though it cried, "I would be possessed by" or "I would possess that which is Human. What do I care if it is good or bad?" There is no "disillusionment," for they have found that which they have sought, but that which they have sought and found is a fragment.

In Memoriam

by *André Gide*

I

Those who came into contact with Wilde only toward the end of his life have a poor notion, from the weakened and broken being whom the prison returned to us, of the prodigious being he was at first. It was in '91 that I met him for the first time. Wilde had at the time what Thackeray calls "the chief gift of great men": success. His gesture, his look triumphed. His success was so certain that it seemed that it preceded Wilde and that all he needed do was go forward to meet it. His books astonished, charmed. His plays were to be the talk of London. He was rich; he was tall; he was handsome; laden with good fortune and honors. Some compared him to an Asiatic Bacchus; others to some Roman emperor; others to Apollo himself—and the fact is that he was radiant.

At Paris, no sooner did he arrive, than his name ran from mouth to mouth; a few absurd anecdotes were related about him: Wilde was still only the man who smoked gold-tipped cigarettes and who walked about in the streets with a sunflower in his hand. For, Wilde, clever at duping the makers of worldly celebrity, knew how to project, beyond his real character, an amusing phantom which he played most spiritedly.

I heard him spoken of at the home of Mallarmé: he was portrayed as a brilliant talker, and I wished to know him, though I had no hope of managing to do so. A happy chance, or rather a friend, to whom I had told my desire, served me. Wilde was invited to

dinner. It was at the restaurant. There were four of us, but Wilde
was the only one who talked.

Wilde did not converse: he narrated. Throughout almost the
whole of the meal, he did not stop narrating. He narrated gently,
slowly; his very voice was wonderful. He knew French admirably,
but he pretended to hunt about a bit for the words which he
wanted to keep waiting. He had almost no accent, or at least only
such as it pleased him to retain and which might give the words a
sometimes new and strange aspect. He was fond of pronouncing
skepticisme for "scepticisme" . . .[1] The tales which he kept telling
us all through the evening were confused and not of his best; Wilde
was uncertain of us and was testing us. Of his wisdom or indeed
of his folly, he uttered only what he believed his hearer would
relish; he served each, according to his appetite, his taste; those who
expected nothing of him had nothing, or just a bit of light froth; and
as his first concern was to amuse, many of those who thought they
knew him knew only the jester in him.

When the meal was over, we left. As my two friends were walking
together, Wilde took me aside:

"You listen with your eyes," he said to me rather abruptly.
"That's why I'm going to tell you this story: When Narcissus died,
the flowers of the field asked the river for some drops of water to
weep for him. 'Oh!' answered the river, 'if all my drops of water
were tears, I should not have enough to weep for Narcissus myself.
I loved him!' 'Oh!' replied the flowers of the field, 'how could you
not have loved Narcissus? He was beautiful.' 'Was he beautiful?'
said the river. 'And who could know better than you? Each day,
leaning over your bank, he beheld his beauty in your water . . .' "

Wilde paused for a moment . . .

" 'If I loved him,' replied the river, 'it was because, when he
leaned over my water, I saw the reflection of my waters in his
eyes.' "

Then Wilde, swelling up with a strange burst of laughter, added,
"That's called *The Disciple.*"

We had arrived at his door and left him. He invited me to see

[1] The *sc* of *scepticisme* (scepticism) is pronounced as though it were *s* alone.—
(Translator's note.)

him again. That year and the following year I saw him often and everywhere.

Before others, as I have said, Wilde wore a showy mask, designed to astonish, amuse, or, at times, exasperate. He never listened, and paid scant heed to ideas as soon as they were no longer his own. As soon as he ceased to shine all by himself, he effaced himself. After that, he was himself again only when one was once more alone with him.

But no sooner alone he would begin:

"What have you done since yesterday?"

And as my life at that time flowed along rather smoothly, the account that I might give of it offered no interest. I would docilely repeat trivial facts, noting, as I spoke, that Wilde's brow would darken.

"Is that really what you've done?"

"Yes," I would answer.

"And what you say is true!"

"Yes, quite true."

"But then why repeat it? You do see that it's not at all interesting. Understand that there are two worlds: the one that *is* without one's speaking about it; it's called the *real world* because there's no need to talk about it in order to see it. And the other is the world of art; that's the one which has to be talked about because it would not exist otherwise.

"There was once a man who was beloved in his village because he would tell stories. Every morning he left the village and in the evening when he returned, all the village workmen, after having drudged all day long, would gather about him and say, 'Come! Tell us! What did you see today?' He would tell: 'I saw a faun in the forest playing a flute, to whose music a troop of woodland creatures were dancing around.' 'Tell us more; what did you see?' said the men. 'When I came to the seashore, I saw three mermaids, at the edge of the waves, combing their green hair with a golden comb.' And the men loved him because he told them stories.

"One morning, as every morning, he left his village—but when he came to the seashore, lo! he beheld three mermaids combing their green hair with a golden comb. And as he continued his walk, he saw, as he came near the woods, a faun playing the flute to a troop of woodland creatures. That evening, when he came back to his village and was asked, as on other evenings, 'Come! Tell us! What did you see?' he answered, 'I saw nothing.' "

Wilde paused for some moments, let the effect of the tale work its way in me, and then resumed, "I don't like your lips; they're straight, like those of someone who has never lied. I want to teach you to lie, so that your lips may become beautiful and twisted like those of an antique mask.

"Do you know what makes the work of art and what makes the work of nature? Do you know what makes them different? For, after all, the flower of the narcissus is as beautiful as a work of art— and what distinguishes them can not be beauty. Do you know what distinguishes them?—The work of art is always *unique*. Nature, which makes nothing durable, always repeats itself so that nothing which it makes may be lost. There are many narcissus flowers; that's why each one can live only a day. And each time that nature invents a new form, she at once repeats it. A sea-monster in a sea knows that in another sea is another sea-monster, his like. When God creates a Nero, a Borgia or a Napoleon in history, he puts another one elsewhere; this one is not known, it little matters; the important thing is that *one* succeed; for God invents man, and man invents the work of art.

"Yes, I know . . . one day there was a great uneasiness on earth, as if nature were at last going to create something unique, something truly unique—and Christ was born on earth. Yes, I know . . . but listen:

"When, in the evening, Joseph of Arimathaea went down from Mount Calvary where Jesus had just died he saw a young man seated on a white stone and weeping. And Joseph approached him and said, 'I understand that your grief is great, for certainly that Man was a just Man.' But the young man answered, 'Oh! that's not why I'm weeping. I'm weeping because I too have performed miracles! I too have restored sight to the blind, I have healed paralytics and I have raised up the dead. I too have withered the barren fig-tree and I have changed water into wine . . . And men have not crucified me.' "

And it seemed to me more than once that Oscar Wilde was convinced of his representative mission.

The Gospel disturbed and tormented the pagan Wilde. He did not forgive it its miracles. The pagan miracle is the work of art: Christianity was encroaching. All robust artistic unrealism requires an earnest realism in life.

His most ingenious apologues, his most disturbing ironies were designed to bring the two ethics face to face with one another, I mean pagan naturalism and Christian idealism, and to put the latter out of countenance.

"When Jesus wished to return to Nazareth," he related, "Nazareth was so changed that He no longer recognized His city. The Nazareth in which He had lived had been full of lamentations and tears; this city was full of bursts of laughter and singing. And Christ, entering the city, saw slaves loaded with flowers hastening toward the marble stairway of a house of white marble. Christ entered the house, and at the rear of a room of jasper He saw lying on a regal couch a man whose disheveled hair was entwined with red roses and whose lips were red with wine. Christ approached him, touched him upon the shoulder and said, 'Why leadest thou this life?' The man turned about, recognized Him and replied, 'I was a leper; Thou hast healed me. Why should I lead another life?'

"Christ went out of that house. And lo! in the street he beheld a woman whose face and garments were painted, and whose feet were shod with pearls; and behind her walked a man whose coat was of two colors and whose eyes were laden with desire. And Christ approached the man, touched him upon the shoulder and said, 'Why dost thou follow that woman and regard her thus?' The man, turning about, recognized Him and replied, 'I was blind; Thou hast healed me. What should I do otherwise with my sight?'

"And Christ approached the woman. 'The road which you follow,' He said to her, 'is that of sin; wherefore follow it?' The woman recognized Him and laughingly said to Him, 'The road which I follow is a pleasing one and Thou hast pardoned me all my sins.'

"Then Christ felt His heart full of sadness and wished to leave that city. But as He was leaving it, He saw at length beside the moats of the city a youth who was weeping. Christ approached him, and touching his locks, said to him, 'My friend, wherefore weepest thou?'

"The youth lifted up his eyes, recognized Him, and replied, 'I was dead and Thou hast raised me up; what should I do otherwise with my life?' "

"Would you like me to tell you a secret?" Wilde began another day—it was at the home of Heredia; he had taken me aside in the midst of a crowded drawing-room—"a secret . . . but promise me not to tell it to anyone . . . Do you know why Christ did not love His mother?" This was spoken into my ear, in a low voice and as if ashamedly. He paused a moment, grasped my arm, drew back, and then bursting into laughter, said, "It's because she was a virgin! . . ."

Let me again be permitted to quote this tale, a most strange one and a tough nut for the mind to crack—it is a rare spirit that will understand the contradiction, which Wilde hardly seems to be inventing.

". . . Then there was a great silence in the Chamber of God's Justice.—And the soul of the sinner advanced stark naked before God.

And God opened the book of the sinner's life:

'Certainly your life has been very bad: You have . . . (followed a prodigious, marvelous enumeration of sins).[2]—Since you have done all that, I am certainly going to send you to Hell.'

'You can not send me to Hell.'

'And why can I not send you to Hell?'

'Because I have lived there all my life.'

Then there was a great silence in the Chamber of God's Justice.

'Well, since I can not send you to Hell, I am going to send you to Heaven.'

'You can not send me to Heaven.'

'And why can I not send you to Heaven?'

'Because I have never been able to imagine it.'

[2] The written version which he later made of this tale is, for a wonder, excellent.

And there was a great silence in the Chamber of God's Justice." [3]

One morning Wilde handed me an article to read in which a rather dull-witted critic congratulated him for "knowing how to invent pleasant tales the better to clothe his thought."

"They believe," Wilde began, "that all thoughts are born naked . . . They don't understand that *I can not* think otherwise than in stories. The sculptor doesn't try to translate his thought into marble; *he thinks in marble, directly.*

"There was a man who could think only in bronze. And one day this man had an idea, the idea of joy, of the joy which dwells in the moment. And he felt that he had to tell it. But in all the world, not a single piece of bronze was left; for men had used it all. And this man felt that he would go mad if he did not tell his idea.

"And he thought about a piece of bronze on the grave of his wife, about a statue he had made to adorn the grave of his wife, of the only woman he had loved; it was the statue of sadness, of the sadness which dwells in life. And the man felt that he would go mad if he did not tell his idea.

"So he took the statue of sadness, of the sadness which dwells in life; he smashed it and made of it the statue of joy, of the joy which dwells only in the moment."

Wilde believed in some sort of fatality of the artist, and that the idea is stronger than the man.

"There are," he would say, "two kinds of artist: one brings answers, and the other, questions. We have to know whether one belongs to those who answer or to those who question; for the kind which questions is never that which answers. There are works which wait, and which one does not understand for a long time; the reason is that they bring answers to questions which have not yet been raised; for the question often arrives a terribly long time after the answer."

And he would also say:

"The soul is born old in the body; it is to rejuvenate it that the latter grows old. Plato is the youth of Socrates . . ."

Then I remained for three years without seeing him again.

[3] Since Villiers de l'Isle-Adam betrayed it, everybody knows, alas! the "great secret of the Church": *There is no Purgatory.*

II

Here begin the tragic memories.

A persistent rumor, growing with each of his successes (in London he was being played at the same time in three theatres), ascribed strange practices to Wilde; some people were so kind as to take umbrage at them with a smile, and others took no umbrage at all; it was claimed moreover that he took no pains to hide them, that, on the contrary, he flaunted them; some said, courageously; others, cynically; others, affectedly. I listened to this rumor with great astonishment. Nothing, since I had been associating with Wilde, could have ever made me suspect a thing.—But already, out of prudence, a number of former friends were deserting him. People were not yet repudiating him outright, but they no longer made much of having met him.

An extraordinary chance brought our two paths together again. It was in January 1895. I was traveling; I was driven to do so by a kind of anxiety, more in quest of solitude than in the novelty of places. The weather was frightful; I had fled from Algiers toward Blidah; I was going to leave Blidah for Biskra. At the moment of leaving the hotel, out of idle curiosity, I looked at the blackboard where the names of the travelers were written. What did I see there? —Beside my name, touching it, that of Wilde . . . I have said that I was longing for solitude: I took the sponge and rubbed out my name.

Before reaching the station, I was no longer quite sure whether a bit of cowardice might not have been hidden in this act; at once, retracing my steps, I had my valise brought up again and rewrote my name on the board.

In the three years that I had not seen him (for I can not count a brief meeting at Florence the year before), Wilde had certainly changed. One felt less softness in his look, something raucous in his laughter and something frenzied in his joy. He seemed both more sure of pleasing and less ambitious to succeed in doing so; he was bolder, stronger, bigger. What was strange was that he no longer spoke in apologues; during the few days that I lingered in his company, I was unable to draw the slightest tale from him.

I was at first astonished at finding him in Algeria.

"Oh!" he said to me, "it's that now I'm fleeing from the work of art; I no longer want to adore anything but the sun . . . Have you noticed that the sun detests thought; it always makes it withdraw and take refuge in the shade. At first, thought lived in Egypt; the sun conquered Egypt. It lived in Greece for a long time, the sun conquered Greece; then Italy and then France. At the present time, all thought finds itself pushed back to Norway and Russia, places where the sun never comes. The sun is jealous of the work of art."

To adore the sun, ah! was to adore life. Wilde's lyrical adoration was growing wild and terrible. A fatality was leading him on; he could not and would not elude it. He seemed to put all his concern, his virtue, into overexaggerating his destiny and losing patience with himself. He went to pleasure as one marches to duty.—"My duty to myself," he would say, "is to amuse myself terrifically."

Nietzsche astonished me less, later on, because I had heard Wilde say:

"Not happiness! Above all, not happiness. Pleasure! We must always want the most tragic . . ."

He would walk in the streets of Algiers, preceded, escorted, followed by an extraordinary band of ragamuffins; he chatted with each one; he regarded them all with joy and tossed his money to them haphazardly.

"I hope," he said to me, "to have quite demoralized this city."

I thought of the word used by Flaubert who, when someone asked him what kind of glory he was most ambitious of, replied, "That of demoralizer."

In the face of all this, I remained full of astonishment, admiration, and fear. I was aware of his shaky situation, the hostilities, the attacks, and what a dark anxiety he hid beneath his bold joy.[4]

[4] One of those last Algiers evenings, Wilde seemed to have promised himself to say nothing serious. . . . I grew somewhat irritated with his too witty paradoxes:

"You've better things to say than witticisms," I began. "You're talking to me this evening as if I were the public. You ought rather talk to the public the way you know how to talk to your friends. Why aren't your plays better? You talk away the best of yourself; why don't you write it down?"

"Oh!" he exclaimed at once, "but my plays are not at all good; and I don't put

He spoke of returning to London; the Marquis of Q . . . was insulting him, summoning him, accusing him of fleeing.

"But if you go back there, what will happen?" I asked him. "Do you know what you're risking?"

"One should never know that . . . They're extraordinary, my friends; they advise prudence. Prudence! But can I have any? That would be going backwards. I must go as far as possible . . . I can not go further . . . Something must happen . . . something else . . ."

Wilde embarked the following day.

The rest of the story is familiar. That "something else" was *hard labor*.[5]

---

any stock in them at all. . . . But if you only knew what amusement they give! . . . Almost every one is the result of a wager. *Dorian Gray* too; I wrote it in a few days because one of my friends claimed that I could never write a novel. It bores me so much, writing!"—Then, suddenly bending over toward me: "Would you like to know the great drama of my life?—It's that I've put my genius into my life; I've put only my talent into my works."

It was only too true. The best of his writing is only a pale reflection of his brilliant conversation. Those who have heard him speak find it disappointing to read him. *Dorian Gray*, at the very beginning, was a splendid story, how superior to the *Peau de Chagrin!* how much more *significant!* Alas! written down, what a masterpiece *manqué.*—In his most charming tales there is too great an intrusion of literature. Graceful as they may be, one feels too greatly the affectation; preciosity and euphuism conceal the beauty of the first invention; one feels in them, one can never stop feeling, the three moments of their genesis; the first idea is quite beautiful, simple, profound and certainly sensational; a kind of latent necessity holds its parts firmly together; but from here on, the gift stops; the development of the parts is carried out factitiously; they are not well organized; and when, afterwards, Wilde works on his phrases, and goes about pointing them up, he does so by a prodigious overloading of concetti, of trivial inventions, which are pleasing and curious, in which emotion stops, with the result that the glittering of the surface makes our mind lose sight of the deep central emotion.

[5] I have invented nothing and arranged nothing in the last remarks I quote. Wilde's words are present to my mind, and I was going to say to my ear. I am not claiming that Wilde clearly saw prison rising up before him; but I do assert that the dramatic turn which surprised and astounded London, abruptly transforming Wilde from accuser to accused, did not, strictly speaking, cause him any surprise. The newspapers, which were unwilling to see anything more in him than a clown, did their best to misrepresent the attitude of his defense, to the point of depriving it of any meaning. Perhaps, in some far-off time it will be well to lift this frightful trial out of its abominable filth.

A Novel by Mr. Oscar Wilde

by Walter Pater

There is always something of an excellent talker about the
writing of Mr. Oscar Wilde; and in his hands, as happens so rarely
with those who practise it, the form of dialogue is justified by its
being really alive. His genial, laughter-loving sense of life and its
enjoyable intercourse, goes far to obviate any crudity there may be
in the paradox, with which, as with the bright and shining truth
which often underlies it, Mr. Wilde, startling his "countrymen,"
carries on, more perhaps than any other writer, the brilliant critical
work of Matthew Arnold. *The Decay of Lying,* for instance, is all
but unique in its half-humorous, yet wholly convinced, presentment
of certain valuable truths of criticism. Conversational ease, the
fluidity of life, felicitous expression, are qualities which have a
natural alliance to the successful writing of fiction; and side by
side with Mr. Wilde's *Intentions* (so he entitles his critical efforts)
comes a novel, certainly original, and affording the reader a fair
opportunity of comparing his practice as a creative artist with many
a precept he has enounced as critic concerning it.

A wholesome dislike of the common-place, rightly or wrongly
identified by him with the *bourgeois,* with our middle-class—its
habits and tastes—leads him to protest emphatically against so-
called "realism" in art; life, as he argues, with much plausibility, as
a matter of fact, when it is really awake, following art—the fashion
an effective artist sets; while art, on the other hand, influential and
effective art, has never taken its cue from actual life. In *Dorian
Gray* he is true certainly, on the whole, to the æsthetic philosophy
of his *Intentions;* yet not infallibly, even on this point: there is a
certain amount of the intrusion of real life and its sordid aspects—

"A Novel by Mr. Oscar Wilde" by Walter Pater. From *The Bookman* (November, 1891).

the low theatre, the pleasures and griefs, the faces of some very un-
refined people, managed, of course, cleverly enough. The interlude
of Jim Vane, his half-sullen but wholly faithful care for his sister's
honour, is as good as perhaps anything of the kind, marked by a
homely but real pathos, sufficiently proving a versatility in the
writer's talent, which should make his books popular. Clever always, this book, however, seems intended to set forth anything but
a homely philosophy of life for the middle-class—a kind of dainty
Epicurean theory, rather—yet fails, to some degree, in this; and
one can see why. A true Epicureanism aims at a complete though
harmonious development of man's entire organism. To lose the
moral sense therefore, for instance, the sense of sin and righteous-
ness, as Mr. Wilde's hero—his heroes are bent on doing as speedily,
as completely as they can, is to lose, or lower, organisation, to become less complex, to pass from a higher to a lower degree of development. As a story, however, a partly supernatural story, it is
first-rate in artistic management; those Epicurean niceties only
adding to the decorative colour of its central figure, like so many
exotic flowers, like the charming scenery, and the perpetual, epigrammatic, surprising, yet so natural, conversations, like an atmosphere all about it. All that pleasant accessory detail, taken straight
from the culture, the intellectual and social interests, the con-
ventionalities, of the moment, have, in fact, after all, the effect of
the better sort of realism, throwing into relief the adroitly-devised
supernatural element after the manner of Poe, but with a grace
he never reached, which supersedes that earlier didactic purpose,
and makes the quite sufficing interest of an excellent story.

We like the hero, and, spite of his, somewhat unsociable, devotion
to his art, Hallward, better than Lord Henry Wotton. He has too
much of a not very really refined world in and about him, and his
somewhat cynic opinions, which seem sometimes to be those of the
writer, who may, however, have intended Lord Henry as a satiric
sketch. Mr. Wilde can hardly have intended him, with his cynic
amity of mind and temper, any more than the miserable end of
Dorian himself, to figure the motive and tendency of a true Cyrenaic
or Epicurean doctrine of life. In contrast with Hallward, the artist,
whose sensibilities idealise the world around him, the personality
of Dorian Gray, above all, into something magnificent and strange,

we might say that Lord Henry, and even more the, from the first, suicidal hero, loses too much in life to be a true Epicurean—loses so much in the way of impressions, of pleasant memories, and subsequent hopes, which Hallward, by a really Epicurean economy, manages to secure. It should be said, however, in fairness, that the writer is impersonal: seems not to have identified himself entirely with any one of his characters: and Wotton's cynicism, or whatever it be, at least makes a very clever story possible. He becomes the spoiler of the fair young man, whose bodily form remains un-aged; while his picture, the *chef d'œuvre* of the artist Hallward, changes miraculously with the gradual corruption of his soul. How true, what a light on the artistic nature, is the following on actual personalities and their revealing influence in art. We quote it as an example of Mr. Wilde's more serious style.

> I sometimes think that there are only two eras of any importance in the world's history. The first is the appearance of a new medium for art, and the second is the appearance of new personality for art also. What the invention of oil painting was to the Venetians, the face of Antinous was to late Greek sculpture, and the face of Dorian Gray will some day be to me. It is not merely that I paint from him, draw from him, sketch from him. Of course I have done all that. But he is much more to me than a model or a sitter. I won't tell you that I am dissatisfied with what I have done of him, or that his beauty is such that Art cannot express it. There is nothing that Art cannot express, and I know that the work I have done, since I met Dorian Gray, is good work, is the best work of my life. But in some curious way his personality has suggested to me an entirely new manner in art, an entirely new mode of style. I see things differently, I think of them differently. I can now re-create life in a way that was hidden from me before.

Dorian himself, though certainly a quite unsuccessful experiment in Epicureanism, in life as a fine art, is (till his inward spoiling takes visible effect suddenly, and in a moment, at the end of his story) a beautiful creation. But his story is also a vivid, though carefully considered, exposure of the corruption of a soul, with a very plain moral, pushed home, to the effect that vice and crime make people coarse and ugly. General readers, nevertheless, will probably care less for this moral, less for the fine, varied, largely appreciative culture of the writer, in evidence from page to page, than for the story itself, with its adroitly managed supernatural incidents, its almost equally wonderful applications of natural science; impossible, surely, in fact, but plausible enough in fiction. Its interest turns on that very old theme, old because based on some inherent experience or fancy of the human brain, of a double life: of Döppelgänger—not of two *persons*, in this case, but of the man and his portrait; the latter of which, as we hinted above, changes, decays, is spoiled, while the former, through a long course of corruption, remains, to the outward eye, unchanged, still in all the beauty of a seemingly immaculate youth—"the devil's bargain." But it would be a pity to spoil the reader's enjoyment by further detail. We need only emphasise, once more, the skill, the real subtlety of art, the ease and fluidity withal of one telling a story by word of mouth, with which the consciousness of the supernatural is introduced into, and maintained amid, the elaborately conventional, sophisticated, disabused world Mr. Wilde depicts so cleverly, so mercilessly. The special fascination of the piece is, of course, just there—at that point of contrast. Mr. Wilde's work may fairly claim to go with that of Edgar Poe, and with some good French work of the same kind, done, probably, in more or less conscious imitation of it.

In Honorem Doriani Creatorisque Eius

by Lionel Johnson

Benedictus sis, Oscare!
Qui me libro hoc dignare
   Propter amicitias:
Modo modulans Romano
Laudes dignas Doriano,
   Ago tibi gratias.

Juventutis hic formosa
Floret inter rosas rosa,
   Subito dum venit mors:
Ecce Homo! ecce Deus!
Si sic modo esset meus
   Genius misericors!

Amat avidus amores
Miros, miros carpit flores
   Sævus pulchritudine:
Quanto anima nigrescit,
Tanto facies splendescit,
   Mendax, sed quam splendide!

Hic sunt poma Sodomorum;
Hic sunt corda vitiorum;
   Et peccata dulcia.
In excelsis et infernis,

"In Honorem Doriani Creatorisque Eius." From *Complete Poems* by Lionel Johnson, ed. Iain Fletcher (London: Unicorn Press, 1953), p. 246.

Tibi sit, qui tanta cernis,
Gloriarum gloria.

LIONELLUS POETA.[1]

All this is Latin for a thousand thanks.

[1] Translation:

In Honor of Dorian and His Creator

Bless you, Oscar, for honoring me with this book for friendship's sake. Expressing in the Roman tongue praises that befit Dorian, I thank you.

This splendid rose of youth blossoms among roses, until death comes abruptly. Behold the man! Behold the God! If only my soul could take his part.

He avidly loves strange loves and, fierce with beauty, he plucks strange flowers. The more sinister his spirit, the more radiant his face, lying—but how splendidly!

Here are apples of Sodom, here are the very hearts of vices, and tender sins. In heaven and hell be glory of glories to you who perceive so much.

LIONEL THE POET

The Destroyer of a Soul

by *Lionel Johnson*

To————.[1]

I hate you with a necessary hate.
First, I sought patience: passionate was she:
My patience turned in very scorn of me,
That I should dare forgive a sin so great,
As this, through which I sit disconsolate;
Mourning for that live soul, I used to see;
Soul of a saint, whose friend I used to be:
Till you came by! a cold, corrupting, fate.

Why come you now? You, whom I cannot cease
With pure and perfect hate to hate? Go, ring
The death-bell with a deep, triumphant toll!
Say you, my friend sits by me still? Ah, peace!
Call you this thing my friend? this nameless thing?
This living body, hiding its dead soul?

[*1892*]

"The Destroyer of a Soul." From *Complete Poems* by Lionel Johnson, ed. Iain Fletcher (London: Unicorn Press, 1953), p. 94.

[1] Probably Oscar Wilde, to whom Johnson introduced Alfred Douglas in 1891.

The Arrest of Oscar Wilde at the Cadogan Hotel

by John Betjeman

He sipped at a weak hock and seltzer
  As he gazed at the London skies
Through the Nottingham lace of the curtains
  Or was it his bees-winged eyes?

To the right and before him Pont Street
  Did tower in her new built red,
As hard as the morning gaslight
  That shone on his unmade bed.

"I want some more hock in my seltzer,
  And Robbie, please give me your hand—
Is this the end or beginning?
  How can I understand?

"So you've brought me the latest *Yellow Book:*
  And Buchan has got in it now:
Approval of what is approved of
  Is as false as a well-kept vow.

"More hock, Robbie—where is the seltzer?
  Dear boy, pull again at the bell!
They are all little better than *cretins,*
  Though this *is* the Cadogan Hotel.

"One astrakhan coat is at Willis's—
  Another one's at the Savoy:

"The Arrest of Oscar Wilde at the Cadogan Hotel." From *Collected Poems* by John Betjeman. (Boston: Houghton Mifflin Company, 1958), p. 17. Reprinted by permission of John Murray, Ltd.

Do fetch my morocco portmanteau,
   And bring them on later, dear boy."

A thump, and a murmur of voices—
   ("Oh why must they make such a din?")
As the door of the bedroom swung open
   And Two Plain Clothes POLICEMEN came in:

"Mr. Woilde, we 'ave come for tew take yew
   Where felons and criminals dwell:
We must ask yew tew leave with us quoietly
   For this *is* the Cadogan Hotel."

He rose, and he put down *The Yellow Book*.
   He staggered—and, terrible-eyed,
He brushed past the palms on the staircase
   And was helped to a hansom outside.

The Dead Poet

by *Alfred Douglas*

I dreamed of him last night, I saw his face
All radiant and unshadowed of distress,
And as of old, in music measureless,
I heard his golden voice and marked him trace
Under the common thing the hidden grace,
And conjure wonder out of emptiness,
Till mean things put on beauty like a dress
And all the world was an enchanted place.

And then methought outside a fast locked gate
I mourned the loss of unrecorded words,
Forgotten tales and mysteries half said,
Wonders that might have been articulate,
And voiceless thoughts like murdered singing birds.
And so I woke and knew that he was dead.

Paris, 1901

Sonnet on Wilde

by *Alfred Douglas*

For I was of the world's top, born to bask
In its preferment where the augurs sit,
And where the devil's grace, to counterfeit,
Is all the tribute that the augurs ask
(Whose wedding-garments is a hood and mask).
But God be praised who still denied me wit
To "play the game" or play the hypocrite
And make a virtue of the devil's task.

I left "the game" to others, and behold,
This same perversion's priest, this lord of lies
Is now exalted on your altar's height;
His sophist's tinsel is acclaimed pure gold,
And England's course, swayed by his votaries,
Declines upon corruption and black night.

Wormwood Scrubs Prison, 1924

"Sonnet on Wilde" (Editor's title). Sonnet XIV from a sequence entitled *In Excelsis* in *The Complete Poems of Lord Alfred Douglas* (London: Martin Secker Ltd., 1928), p. 130. Copyright 1928 by Martin Secker Ltd. Reprinted by permission of Martin Secker & Warburg, Ltd.

C 33

by Hart Crane

He has woven rose-vines
About the empty heart of night,
And vented his long mellowed wines
Of dreaming on the desert white
With searing sophistry.
And he tented with far truths he would form
The transient bosoms from the thorny tree.

O Materna! to enrich thy gold head
And wavering shoulders with a new light shed

From penitence must needs bring pain,
And with it song of minor, broken strain.
But you who hear the lamp whisper thru night
Can trace paths tear-wet, and forget all blight.

Fiction as Allegory:
The Picture of Dorian Gray

by Edouard Roditi

From the eighteenth-century vogue of Ann Radcliffe and Horace Walpole to the success, in the early decades of the nineteenth century, of the novels of "Monk" Lewis, a whole literary genre had culminated, in 1820, in the publication of *Melmoth the Wanderer*. Its author, Charles Robert Maturin, was, by marriage, an uncle of Wilde's mother, the poetess Speranza. Wilde knew *Melmoth* well, and was proud of this relationship. When the old novel was reprinted in 1892 with a long biographical introduction, the editors expressed their thanks, in a preface, "to Mr. Oscar Wilde and Lady Wilde (Speranza) for details with regard to Maturin's life." And when Wilde retired to France after his release from Reading Gaol, he lived there under the name of Sebastian Melmoth which he used as a pseudonym until his death. From Reading Gaol, in a letter to Robert Ross dated April 6th, 1897, Wilde wrote, of Rossetti's letters which he had just read and considered forgeries, that he had been interested, "to see how my grand-uncle's *Melmoth* and my mother's *Sidonia* have been two books that fascinated his youth." Though certainly ignorant of Lautréamont's passion for the Satanic wanderer, Wilde surely knew that Baudelaire had praised *Melmoth* in *De l'Essence du Rire*; and he was proud of the high esteem in which two of his favorite authors, Byron and Balzac, had held his mother's uncle.

Of Maturin's influence on Wilde we have ample proof. Maturin's biographers state that "he always showed an extravagant taste for dressing up" and that "throughout his life a love of masquerade and theatrical display never deserted him." His eccentricities of dress were noted, besides, by many contemporaries: Byron described him, in a letter, as "a bit of a coxcomb." Speranza likewise attracted much attention, in Dublin society and later in London, by her none too tasteful splendors, recorded by several contemporaries. Wilde's own sartorial extravagances thus seem to have been inspired to some extent by a family weakness, though a well-established tradition of dandyism, from the age of Byron and Maturin, through that of Bulwer Lytton and Disraeli, still encouraged the affectations of a Brummel among artists of Wilde's generation.

Much as Wilde may have been influenced, in his art and his life, by the more dandified Romanticism of such novels as Bulwer Lytton's *Pelham* or Disraeli's *Vivian Grey* and *Lothair,* with their epigrammatic brilliance and foppish haughtiness inherited from the Regency bucks, there is also, in *The Picture of Dorian Gray,* distinct evidence of direct borrowings from *Melmoth.* In the opening chapter of Maturin's novel, when Melmoth, the young student, comes to his miserly uncle's death-bed, he is sent to fetch some wine from a closet "which no foot but that of old Melmoth had entered for nearly sixty years." There, amidst "a great deal of decayed and useless lumber" such as that which later furnished the locked and abandoned school-room where Dorian Gray concealed his compromising portrait, young Melmoth's eyes were "in a moment, and as if by magic, riveted on a portrait" whose eyes "were such as one feels they wish they had never seen, and feels they can never forget." This portrait represents an evil ancestor, a third Melmoth who, by a pact with the devil, has been permitted to live one hundred and fifty years without showing any signs of aging, much as Dorian Gray was mysteriously permitted to retain the appearance of his youth in spite of his crimes and debauchery. And this ancestor, Melmoth the Wanderer, is still alive: fear of him has even caused the old miser's death.

Maturin's whole romance then unfolds as a tangled series of episodes from the Wanderer's legendary life. And when, in the last pages, the evil ancestor returns to the place of his birth because "the clock of eternity is about to strike," in his last moments of life he suddenly ages: "the lines of extreme age were visible in every feature. His hairs were as white as snow, his mouth had fallen in, the muscles of his face were relaxed and withered—he was the very image of hoary decrepit debility."

The magic formula of Dorian Gray's sinister youth was thus an heirloom in Wilde's family, handed down like some choice recipe from old Maturin, from one of the sources of the Dracula myth in novels and movies to the author of *The Picture of Dorian Gray* which, when it was finally filmed, was acclaimed by the poet Parker Tyler as "the last of the movie Draculas." And Dorian Gray himself, whose mere presence, as his lasting youth became more and more sinister, would "make a man like the Duke of Berwick leave the room," whose friendship "was so fatal to young men," is a half-brother of Lautréamont's Maldoror. The arch-fiend of Surrealist satanism is indeed but another scion of the same Melmoth who boasts: "It has been reported of me, that I obtained from the enemy of souls a range of existence beyond the period allotted to mortality—a power to pass over space without disturbance or delay, and visit remote regions with the swiftness of thought—to encounter tempests without the *hope* of their blasting me, and penetrate dungeons whose bolts were as flax and tow at my touch."

From Melmoth, Dorian Gray thus inherited his lasting youth, and Maldoror his gift of ubiquity, of travel without disturbance or delay, and "that singular expression of the features (the eyes particularly), which no human glance could meet unappalled." But both of these Draculas outdid, in one respect, their ghoulish sire. The Reverend Maturin, a worthy Anglican minister with what even a snob in a Somerset Maugham novel calls "a good old Irish name," was apparently unwilling to permit his monster to lead any victims to damnation. And as he is about to die, the Wanderer exclaims: "No one has ever exchanged destinies with Melmoth the Wanderer. *I have traversed the world in the search, and no one, to gain that world, would lose his own soul.*" Maldoror and Dorian Gray, however, were both more successful as tempters, and each of them left a trail of blasted lives behind him.

The portrait concealed in Melmoth's closet is bound to the ghoulish wanderer by no such ties of sympathetic magic as those which bind Dorian Gray to his portrait; it occupies no such central position in Maturin's story and remains a mere accessory which is destroyed, without dire consequences, shortly after it is discovered, so that one barely remembers it as one reads the rest of the romance. Between its literary avatars in *Melmoth* and in *Dorian Gray*, this portrait had indeed undergone a strange metamorphosis, under the influence of the magical portrait, as Richard Aldington has pointed out, of Max Rodenstein in Benjamin Disraeli's *Vivian Grey*, published in 1826, and also of the magical skin in *La Peau de Chagrin*, written by Balzac in the period in which he was most deeply affected by his readings of Maturin, only a couple of years before he wrote his sequel to the Wanderer's tale, *Melmoth Reconcilié à l'Eglise*. Dorian Gray's portrait is thus born of the Wanderer's, but by Disraeli's miraculous portrait of an incidental character in *Vivian Grey*; and it inherited its central position in Wilde's novel from Balzac's magical skin, together with analogous qualities which reveal themselves just as accidentally and prove just as dire a source of temptation.

As a macabre novel, in spite of this noble ancestry, *The Picture of Dorian Gray* is not entirely successful. The thread of its narrative is too frequently interrupted by Wilde's esthetic preaching, by useless displays of esthetic erudition, by unnecessary descriptions of works of art and by paradoxical table-talk which have little bearing on the plot, except where Lord Henry dazzles and convinces Dorian. The conversation, at times, even distorts the plot. It allows a vague number of duchesses and other characters, doomed to vanish almost immediately after their first appearance, to wander into Wilde's novel, straight from the pages of *Vivian Grey* or of *Pelham*, in a frenzy of brilliant repartee and shrill laughter like the extras who suddenly give life to a court-scene in an old-fashioned light-opera. Between these pauses, where the atmosphere has been slapped on so thick that it clogs the machinery of plot, Wilde's plot itself reveals several curious weaknesses; had not the book been so hastily written that it is almost unjust to analyze it as if it were a carefully devised work of art, these weaknesses would suggest an unexpected mixture, in the author, of amateurishness and prudish guilt-feelings.

Wilde's naïvely romantic descriptions of low life, for instance, are full of pathetic echoes of the melodrama of earlier decades, of De Quincey's years of misery in the London slums where he met

Ann, of the drug-addict poet James Thomson's *The City of Dreadful Night* and even of Charles Dickens; and they contrast oddly with Wilde's infinitely more sophisticated and knowing descriptions of high society. When Wilde's young men with perfect profiles stop flinging themselves petulantly upon the divans of their extravagantly furnished bachelor quarters or dining out with duchesses in a haze of epigrams, they stalk forth, as Vivian Grey or Lothair had done some decades earlier in their moments of tension or despair, into the vast wilderness of London. And there, in the night, Wilde's dandies discover another world, whence they return, at dawn, with "a dim memory of wandering through a labyrinth of sordid houses, of being lost in a giant web of sombre streets" or of "narrow shameful alleys."

Victor Hugo's *Les Misérables* and Eugène Sue's *Les Mystères de Paris* had contributed much to Wilde's romantic vision of London's nocturnal underworld, with its grisly prostitutes, its drunken brawls before the doors of degraded dockland taverns, its foul opium-dens and its sinister Jewish theater-owner like De Quincey's money-lenders or the hideous Jews of Rowlandson's cartoons. All the props, save the sewers, of Victor Hugo's Paris had been imported to England in such popular melodramas of the Seventies as *The Streets of London* or *London by Gaslight*; and it is from this naïve panorama of the sinful city that Wilde's young men at last emerge in Covent Garden, among the vegetables glistening in the dawn light and the rustics who, "rude as they were, with their heavy, hobnailed shoes, and their awkward gait . . . brought a little of Arcady with them."

Between these two worlds, no decent or comfortable middle class, no quiet family life, no dormitory sections in Wilde's vision of the big city. From the brilliantly lit society with which the author seems so well acquainted, we step straight into a dim slum-land of which he seems ignorant, scared or ashamed, whose denizens are all stock characters from almost "gothic" melodrama, like Sybil Vane's mother in *Dorian Gray*, living in a poverty almost too proverbial to be convincing. And it is perhaps significant that Marcel Proust, who translated Ruskin into French and was influenced by his thought even more than Wilde, likewise neglected, in general, to describe, except his own family, a mean of people who live and work decently, between the maximum of the idle Guermantes world, with its dependent servants and its less brilliant gate-crashers such as the Verdurin set and Madame Cottard, and the minimum of Jupien's den of prostitution.

In his handling of crime too, Wilde seems just as ill at ease and inhibited as in his descriptions of the surroundings of crime and poverty. The Reverend Maturin, in *Melmoth the Wanderer,* had never been able to bring himself to write the exact terms of the pact that his satanic character offered to his prospective victims: "Every night he besets me, and few like me could have resisted his seductions. He has offered, and proved to me, that it is in his power to bestow all that human cupidity could thirst for, on the condition that—I cannot utter! It is one so full of horror and impiety that, even to listen to it, is scarce less a crime than to comply with it!" In *Dorian Gray,* Wilde likewise refrains from ever revealing the exact nature of Dorian's evil influence on the many friends, such as Adrian Singleton or Alan Campbell, whose lives his friendship has irremediably seared; and even when Dorian blackmails Alan into helping him dispose of the murdered painter's corpse, he writes "something" on a paper and hands it to Alan, "something" that makes Alan shudder and comply, but that is never revealed to the reader. Such a curious blockage, in both Maturin and Wilde, can suggest, to the psychoanalytically inclined reader, only a crime which is terribly repressed by the prejudices of the age, perhaps what Lord Alfred Douglas called "the Love that dare not speak its name." And Wilde's unwillingness to name this sin in *Dorian Gray* makes one all the more sceptical of his authorship of *The Priest and the Acolyte,* a strangely sacrilegious and outspoken story which is sometimes attributed to Wilde and, though it handles Wilde's favorite theme of "each man kills the thing he loves," contains none of his ubiquitous paradoxes and epigrams. At the time of Wilde's trial, it was moreover proved conclusively that he had not written *The Priest and the Acolyte,* nor ever met its author, an obscure Oxford undergraduate.

Wilde's unwillingness to handle the details of vice, crime and the underworld as firmly and realistically as he does those of the world of fashion is indeed more than a mere concession to Victorian prudery. He shrinks from it, in his art if not in his life, with the neurotic's resistance, as if from a confession or from the discovery of a maëlstrom of experience into which, as in the tempting visions of *The Sphinx*, he fears being irretrievably drawn. And this squeamishness imposes, on the plot of his novel, some odd distortions which the more objective author of an ordinary mystery-novel would easily have avoided. When Dorian Gray, for instance, seeks "to cure the soul by means of the senses, and the senses by means of the soul," he presses a spring in a cabinet in his home and thus releases a secret drawer where he keeps a box of an unnamed "green paste waxy in lustre, the odour curiously heavy and persistent." This paste is opium; but Dorian Gray, unlike all addicts who always have their pipes at home even if they occasionally run out of "junk," has the opium, it seems, but no pipes. Putting his good opium back in the secret drawer, he therefore rushes out into the night, takes a cab and goes far into London's dockland, to a low den frequented by sailors and derelicts where the "junk" is surely inferior to what he left at home.

Why this unlikely twist in the novel's plot? The habits of opium-addicts were probably little known to Wilde, and Dorian Gray had to be brought somehow to dockland in order to be recognized there by dead Sybil Vane's avenging sailor-brother. But James Vane is then so clumsy in shadowing Dorian that he follows him onto a moor, in the midst of a shooting-party, and gets killed accidentally, as he hides behind a bush, by a shot aimed at a hare! This whole episode of frustrated revenge is thus introduced by means of one unlikely scene and resolved in another; and the awkward lack of verisimilitude of its beginning and end reveals Wilde's ignorance and fear of a world of crime with which, in real life, he was doomed to become all too familiar.

In spite of its many weaknesses, *The Picture of Dorian Gray* yet remains, in many respects, a great novel. Though hastily written and clumsily constructed, it manages to haunt many readers with vivid memories of its visionary descriptions. As a masterpiece of the macabre, it is infinitely less diffuse or rhetorical, and told with more economy and fewer tangles and snappings of the thread of narrative, than *Melmoth the Wanderer*. Wilde had indeed profited by the art of Balzac and Flaubert; and when he revived the obsolete genre of the "gothic" or sartorial novel, he avoided much of the formlessness of *Melmoth*, *The Monk* or *Vivian Grey*, so that Wilde's tale now reads better than most of its literary ancestors and conforms more exactly to our stricter and more sober standards of plot, of atmosphere and of probability for the improbable.

But the true greatness of *The Picture of Dorian Gray* resides in the philosophical doctrine which the novel is intended, as a myth, to illustrate. The *Erziehungsroman* of dandyism pretended to instruct the nineteenth-century reader much as Lord Chesterfield had once taught his son, but in a more fictional form, better suited to the tastes of an age which had outgrown even the eighteenth-century taste for the epistolary novel. As a genre, it produced, in England, four resounding successes: *Tremaine,* by Robert Plumer Ward in 1825, Disraeli's *Vivian Grey* in 1826, Bulwer Lytton's *Pelham* in 1828 and, half a century later, *The Picture of Dorian Gray* in 1890. For all its success, *Tremaine* has little doctrine beyond a pious conformism or conservatism and is of no interest today; both *Vivian Grey* and *Pelham* refer to it sarcastically as a favorite among fashionable women. The doctrine of Disraeli's youthful work, for all its refined tastes in Romantic art and scenery, was one of brashly unscrupulous ambition. In his machiavellian intrigues, Vivian was guided by immediately practical considerations; as a more businesslike and less foolish Beau Brummel, he failed to achieve his ends, though he accepted all the corrupt standards of his society, only because he found himself pitted against Mrs. Felix Lorraine, an even more unscrupulous enemy. Bulwer Lytton's novel portrays a "man of fashion" who is saved, by his intellect and his more fastidious moral judgment, from being corrupted by the fashionable society in which he is so successful; *Pelham* portrays Brummel, in Russelton, as a man who came to grief not so much because he failed to manage his affairs according to the principles of the world of fashion as because he lacked the sound sense of values which only a more intellectual or prudential attitude toward life can provide.

The ethical message of *The Picture of Dorian Gray,* though rarely understood because rarely sought, is no less clear than that which Bulwer Lytton explained in his preface. Lord Henry, Wilde's perfect dandy, expounds to Dorian a paradoxical philosophy of dandyism which shocks Basil Halward but appeals to the young narcissist. In the passion of his self-love, Dorian Gray distorts this doctrine and becomes a fallen dandy, corrupting all those who accompany him along his path and murdering his conscience, Basil Halward; finally, in self-inflicted death, Dorian meets the punishment of excessive self-love. But Lord Henry's true doctrine, more spiritually and less prudentially intellectual than Pelham's, was a philosophy of inaction: beyond good and evil, for all his evil-sounding paradoxes which only illustrate the Taoist identity of contraries where both conscience and temptation are placed on the same footing but then transcended, Lord Henry never acts and never falls.

Oscar Wilde: The Poet of *Salome*

by James Joyce

Oscar Fingal O'Flahertie Wills Wilde. These were the high-sounding titles that with youthful haughtiness he had printed on the title-page of his first collection of poems, and in this proud gesture, by which he tried to achieve nobility, are the signs of his vain pretences and the fate which already awaited him. His name symbolizes him: Oscar, nephew of King Fingal and the only son of Ossian in the amorphous Celtic *Odyssey,* who was treacherously killed by the hand of his host as he sat at table. O'Flahertie, a savage Irish tribe whose destiny it was to assail the gates of medieval cities; a name that incited terror in peaceful men, who still recite, among the plagues, the anger of God, and the spirit of fornication, in the ancient litany of the saints: "from the wild O'Flaherties, libera nos Domine." Like that other Oscar, he was to meet his public death in the flower of his years as he sat at table, crowned with false vine leaves and discussing Plato. Like that savage tribe, he was to break the lance of his fluent paradoxes against the body of practical conventions, and to hear, as a dishonoured exile, the choir of the just recite his name together with that of the unclean.

Wilde was born in the sleepy Irish capital fifty-five years ago. His father was a ranking scientist, who has been called the father of modern otology. His mother, who took part in the literary-revolutionary movement of '48, wrote for the Nationalist newspaper under the pseudonym "Speranza," and incited the public, in her poems and articles, to seize Dublin Castle. There are circumstances regarding the pregnancy of Lady Wilde and the infancy of her son which, in the eyes of some, explain in part the unhappy mania (if it may be called that) which later dragged him to his ruin;[1] and at least it is certain that the child grew up in an atmosphere of insecurity and prodigality.

The public life of Oscar Wilde began at Oxford University, where, at the time of his matriculation, a pompous professor named Ruskin was leading a crowd of Anglo-Saxon adolescents to the promised land of the future society—behind a wheelbarrow.[2] His mother's susceptible temperament revived in the young man, and, beginning with himself, he resolved to put into practice a theory of beauty that was partly original and partly derived from the books of Pater and Ruskin. He provoked the jeers of the public by proclaiming and practising a reform in dress and in the appearance of the home. He made lecture tours in the United States and the English provinces and became the spokesman of the aesthetic school, while around him was forming the fantastic legend of the Apostle of Beauty. His name evoked in the public mind a vague idea of delicate pastels, of life beautified with flowers. The cult of the sunflower, his favourite flower, spread among the leisured class, and the little people heard tell of his famous white ivory walking stick glittering with turquoise stones, and of his Neronian hair-dress.

The subject of this shining picture was more miserable than the bourgeois thought. From time to time his medals, trophies of his academic youth, went to the pawnshop, and at times the young wife of the epigrammatist had to borrow from a neighbour the money for a pair of shoes. Wilde was constrained to accept a position as editor of a very petty newspaper,[3] and only with the presentation of his brilliant comedies did he enter the short last phase of his life—luxury and wealth. *Lady Windermere's Fan* took London by storm. In the tradition of the Irish writers of comedy that runs from the days of Sheridan and Goldsmith to Bernard Shaw,

---

[1] Lady Wilde badly wanted her second child to be a girl, and was disappointed when Oscar was born.

[2] Ruskin set his pupils to work making a road to show the value of communal effort.

[3] *The Woman's World.*

> Wilde became, like them, court jester to the English. He became
the standard of elegance in the metropolis, and the annual income
from his writings reached almost half a million francs. He scattered
his gold among a series of unworthy friends. Every morning he
bought two expensive flowers, one for himself and one for his
coachman; and until the day of his sensational trial, he was driven
to the courtroom in a two-horse carriage with its brilliantly out-
fitted coachman and powdered page.

His fall was greeted by a howl of puritanical joy. At the news of
his condemnation, the crowd gathered outside the courtroom began
to dance a pavane in the muddy street. Newspaper reporters were
admitted to the prison, and through the window of his cell fed on
the spectacle of his shame. White bands covered up his name on
theatre billboards. His friends abandoned him. His manuscripts
were stolen, while he recounted in prison the pain inflicted on him
by two years of forced labour. His mother died under a shadow. His
wife died. He was declared bankrupt and his goods were sold at
auction. His sons were taken from him. When he got out of prison,
thugs urged on by the noble Marquis of Queensbury[4] were waiting
in ambush for him. He was hunted from house to house as dogs
hunt a hare. One after another drove him from the door, refusing
him food and shelter, and at nightfall he finally ended up under
the windows of his brother, weeping and babbling like a child.

The epilogue came rapidly to an end, and it is not worth the
effort to follow the unhappy man from the slums of Naples to his
poor lodgings in the Latin Quarter where he died from meningitis
in the last month of the last year of the nineteenth century.[5] It is
not worth the effort to shadow him, as the French spies did. He
died a Roman Catholic, adding another facet to his public life by
the repudiation of his wild doctrine. After having mocked the idols
of the market place, he bent his knees, sad and repentant that he
had once been the singer of the divinity of joy, and closed the book
of his spirit's rebellion with an act of spiritual dedication.

This is not the place to examine the strange problem of the life
of Oscar Wilde, nor to determine to what extent heredity and the

[4] Father of Lord Alfred Douglas.
[5] Actually, on November 30, 1900.

epileptic tendency of his nervous system can excuse that which has been imputed to him. Whether he was innocent or guilty of the charges brought against him, he undoubtedly was a scapegoat. His greater crime was that he had caused a scandal in England, and it is well known that the English authorities did everything possible to persuade him to flee before they issued an order for his arrest. An employee of the Ministry of Internal Affairs stated during the trial that, in London alone, there are more than 20,000 persons under police surveillance, but they remain footloose until they provoke a scandal. Wilde's letters to his friends were read in court, and their author was denounced as a degenerate obsessed by exotic perversions: "Time wars against you; it is jealous of your lilies and your roses," "I love to see you wandering through violet-filled valleys, with your honey-coloured hair gleaming." But the truth is that Wilde, far from being a perverted monster who sprang in some inexplicable way from the civilization of modern England, is the logical and inescapable product of the Anglo-Saxon college and university system, with its secrecy and restrictions.

Wilde's condemnation by the English people arose from many complex causes; but it was not the simple reaction of a pure conscience. Anyone who scrutinizes the graffiti, the loose drawings, the lewd gestures of those people will hesitate to believe them pure at heart. Anyone who follows closely the life and language of men, whether in soldiers' barracks or in the great commercial houses, will hesitate to believe that all those who threw stones at Wilde were themselves spotless. In fact, everyone feels uncomfortable in speaking to others about this subject, afraid that his listener may know more about it than he does. Oscar Wilde's own defence in the *Scots Observer*[6] should remain valid in the judgment of an objective critic. Everyone, he wrote, sees his own sin in Dorian Gray (Wilde's best known novel). What Dorian Gray's sin was no one says and no one knows. Anyone who recognizes it has committed it.

Here we touch the pulse of Wilde's art—sin. He deceived himself into believing that he was the bearer of good news of neo-paganism

[6] "Mr. Wilde's Rejoinder," *Scots Observer*, v. 4, no. 86 (July 12, 1890) 279, a reply to an unfavourable review of *The Picture of Dorian Gray*. Wilde wrote: "Each man sees his own sin in Dorian Gray. What Dorian Gray's sins are no one knows. He who finds them has brought them."

to an enslaved people. His own distinctive qualities, the qualities, perhaps, of his race—keenness, generosity, and a sexless intellect— he placed at the service of a theory of beauty which, according to him, was to bring back the Golden Age and the joy of the world's youth. But if some truth adheres to his subjective interpretations of Aristotle, to his restless thought that proceeds by sophisms rather than syllogisms, to his assimilations of natures as foreign to his as the delinquent is to the humble, at its very base is the truth inherent in the soul of Catholicism: that man cannot reach the divine heart except through that sense of separation and loss called sin.[7]

In his last book, *De Profundis,* he kneels before a gnostic Christ, resurrected from the apocryphal pages of *The House of Pome-granates,* and then his true soul, trembling, timid, and saddened, shines through the mantle of Heliogabalus. His fantastic legend, his opera[8]—a polyphonic variation on the rapport of art and nature, but at the same time a revelation of his own psyche—his brilliant books sparkling with epigrams (which made him, in the view of some people, the most penetrating speaker of the past century), these are now divided booty.

A verse from the book of Job is cut on his tombstone in the impoverished cemetery at Bagneux. It praises his facility, "eloquium suum,"—the great legendary mantle which is now divided booty. Perhaps the future will also carve there another verse, less proud but more pious:

> *Partiti sunt sibi vestimenta mea et super*
> *vestem meam miserunt sortis.*[9]

---

[7] Compare Aherne in Yeats's *Tables of the Law,* which Joyce knew by heart: "and in my misery it was revealed to me that man can only come to that Heart through the sense of separation from it which we call sin."

[8] Salome.

[9] Psalms 21:19, which reads, "*Diviserunt* sibi . . . miserunt *sortem.*"

Wilde as a Dramatist

by St. John Hankin

The difficulty about Wilde as a playwright was that he never quite got through the imitative phase. *The Importance of Being Earnest* is the nearest approach to absolute originality that he attained. In that play, for the first time, he seemed to be tearing himself away from tradition and to be evolving a dramatic form of his own. Unhappily it was the last play he was to write, and so the promise in it was never fulfilled. Had his career not been cut short at this moment, it is possible that this might have proved the starting-point of a whole series of "Trivial Comedies for Serious People," and that thenceforward Wilde would have definitely discarded the machine-made construction of the Scribe-Sardou theatre which had held him too long, and begun to use the drama as an artist should, for the expression of his own personality, not the manufacture of clever *pastiches*. It would then have become possible to take him seriously as a dramatist. For, paradoxical as it may sound in the case of so merry and light-hearted a play, *The Importance of Being Earnest* is artistically the most serious work that Wilde produced for the theatre. Not only is it by far the most brilliant of his plays considered as literature. It is also the most sincere. With all its absurdity, its psychology is truer, its criticism of life subtler and more profound than that of the other plays. And even in its technique it shows, in certain details, a breaking away from the conventional well-made play of the 'seventies and 'eighties in favour of the looser construction and more naturalistic methods of the newer school.

Consider its "curtains" for a moment and compare them with

"Wilde as a Dramatist" (Editor's title). From *The Dramatic Works of St. John Hankin*, Vol. III (London: Martin Secker, Ltd., 1912), 185–201. Reprinted by permission of Martin Secker & Warburg Limited.

those of the conventional farce or comedy of their day or of Wilde's other plays. In the other plays Wilde clung tenaciously to the old-fashioned "strong" curtain, and I am bound to say he used it with great cleverness, though the cleverness seems to me deplorably wasted. The curtain of the third act of *Lady Windermere's Fan*, when Mrs. Erlynne suddenly emerges from Lord Darlington's inner room, and Lady Windermere, taking advantage of the confusion, glides from her hiding-place in the window and makes her escape unseen, is theatrically extremely effective. So is that of the third act of *An Ideal Husband*, when Mrs. Chieveley triumphantly carries off Lady Chiltern's letter under the very eyes of Lord Goring, who cannot forcibly stop her because his servant enters at that moment in answer to her ring. It is a purely theatrical device only worthy of a popular melodrama. But it produces the requisite thrill in the theatre. On the analogy of these plays one would expect to find in *The Importance of Being Earnest* the traditional "curtains" of well-made farce, each act ending in what used to be called a "tableau" of comic bewilderment or terror or indignation. Instead of this we have really no "curtains" at all. Acts I and II end in the casual, go-as-you-please fashion of the ultra-naturalistic school. They might be the work of Mr. Granville Barker. Of course, there is nothing really go-as-you-please about them save in form. They are as carefully thought out, as ingenious in the best sense, as the strong "curtain" could possibly be. But this will not appear to the superficial observer, who will probably believe that these acts "end anyhow." Here is the end of Act I:

> *Algernon.* Oh, I'm a little anxious about poor Bunbury, that is all.
> *Jack.* If you don't take care, your friend Bunbury will get you into a serious scrape some day.
> *Algernon.* I love scrapes. They are the only things that are never serious.
> *Jack.* Oh, that's nonsense, Algy. You never talk anything but nonsense.
> *Algernon.* Nobody ever does.

> *(Curtain.)*

This may seem an easy, slap-dash method of ending an act, and one which anybody can accomplish, but it is very far from being so easy as it looks. To make it effective in the theatre—and in *The Importance of Being Earnest* it is enormously effective—requires at least as much art as the more elaborate devices of the earlier comedies. Only in this case it is the art which conceals art which is required, not the art which obtrudes it.

In *The Importance of Being Earnest*, in fact, Wilde really invented a new type of play, and that type was the only quite original thing he contributed to the English stage. In form it is farce, but in spirit and in treatment it is comedy. Yet it is not farcical comedy. Farcical comedy is a perfectly well recognised class of drama and a fundamentally different one. There are only two other plays which I can think of which belong to the same type—*Arms and the Man* and *The Philanderer*. *Arms and the Man*, like *The Importance of Being Earnest*, is psychological farce, the farce of ideas. In it Mr. Shaw, like Wilde, has taken the traditional farcical form—the last acts of both plays are quite on traditional lines in their mechanism —and breathed into it a new spirit. Similarly, *The Philanderer* is psychological farce, though here there is less farce and more psychology. Unluckily, the Court performances of this play were marked by a dismal slowness and a portentous solemnity by which its freakish humour and irresponsibility were hidden away out of sight, and its true character completely obscured. Properly played, it would prove, I believe, one of the most amusing and delightful things in Mr. Shaw's theatre.

Having spoken of the most original of Wilde's plays, let me turn now to the least original, to the one in which his imitative faculty finds its fullest expression, *The Duchess of Padua*. *The Duchess of Padua* is a really remarkable example of this faculty. I may add that it is also an extremely amusing one, though the humour is, I suspect, wholly unconscious. It is a tragedy planned on the most ambitious Elizabethan lines, though a certain concession to Mid-Victorian theatrical conventions is made in the way of "strong" curtains. In all other ways it follows its models with touching fidelity. Here you have the swelling rhetoric, the gorgeous imagery, the piling up of the agony, of Webster himself. There is the magniloquent verse for the nobles and the homely prose for the populace to which Shakespeare has accustomed us. First and Second Citizen speak with all the traditional imbecility. The croaking raven bellows for revenge. His name in this case is Moranzone. There is a court scene in the manner of *The Merchant of Venice*. In fact, there is everything which one might count on finding in the play of a genuine Elizabethan—except originality. That, unluckily, is absent. *The Duchess of Padua*, in fact, is an exercise, a study in style, not an authentic work of art. Indeed, there are moments when it is not merely a study but something dangerously like a parody. Here is an example. It comes from the opening scene of the fourth act:

> *Moranzone.* Is the Duke dead?
> *Second Citizen.* He has a knife in his heart, which they say is not healthy for any man.
> *Moranzone.* Who is accused of having killed him?
> *Second Citizen.* Why, the prisoner, sir.
> *Moranzone.* But who is the prisoner?
> *Second Citizen.* Why, he that is accused of the Duke's murder.
> *Moranzone.* I mean, what is his name?
> *Second Citizen.* Faith, the same which his godfathers gave him: what else should it be?

This kind of thing is quite amusing as a skit, but it is a little out of place in a serious tragedy.

And some of the blank verse passages are equally funny, with their elaborate reproduction of the best Elizabethan manner, though here the humour is subtler:

> *Guido.* Let me find mercy when I go at night
> And do foul murder.
> *Duchess.* Murder did you say?
> Murder is hungry, and still cries for more,
> And Death, his brother, is not satisfied,
> But walks the house, and will not go away,
> Unless he has a comrade! Tarry, Death,
> For I will give thee a most faithful lackey
> To travel with thee! Murder, call no more,
> For thou shalt eat thy fill. There is a storm
> Will break upon this house before the morning
> So horrible, that the white moon already
> Turns grey and sick with terror, the low wind
> Goes moaning round the house, and the high stars
> Run madly through the vaulted firmament,

As though the night wept tears of liquid fire
For what the day shall look upon. O weep
Thou lamentable heaven! Weep thy fill!
Though sorrow like a cataract drench the fields,
And make the earth one bitter lake of tears,
It would not be enough.   [*A peal of thunder.*
Do you not hear?
There is artillery in the heavens to-night.
Vengeance is wakened up, and has unloosed
His dogs upon the world, and in this matter
Which lies between us two let him who draws
The thunder on his head beware the ruin
Which the forked flame brings after.
Guido. Away! Away!

Would Webster or Cyril Tournour do it differently? Or any better for that matter? I think not. *The Duchess of Padua* is a school exercise, a set of Latin verses, as it were, constructed after the best Ovidian models, but it is the exercise of a very exceptional schoolboy. And though all of it is imitative and some of it is absurd, it has from the theatrical standpoint very real merits. It is not great drama in any sense, but it would be very effective on the stage—which, after all, is what plays are meant to be. It has a good harrowing plot, plenty of "thrills," plenty of declamation, and plenty of impassioned love-making, everything, in fact, which makes for success with the romantic playgoer. The principal characters, too, except the Duke, who is frankly ridiculous, are well drawn after their kind. Not subtly drawn, of course—subtlety would be thrown away in work of this kind—but drawn clearly and boldly. Some of the verse is really fine, and none of it sinks below a respectable level. Altogether, as the work of quite a young man it is creditable enough. If all the blank verse dramas which have graced the English stage during the past ten years had been half as good, the discerning critic would have had less to complain of.

The Duchess of Padua, in fact, is quite good second-rate work. But as soon as you compare it with first-rate work the poverty of its texture at once becomes obvious. Browning, in *A Soul's Tragedy*—I think his best, because his most characteristic and individual play—took a subject belonging to much the same period as *The Duchess*

of Padua. His scene also is mediæval Italy where cities groan under
the tyranny of their rulers and worldly ecclesiastics pull the strings
of government. But where Wilde could only turn out a clever copy
of other men's work, Browning produced an entirely original type of
drama, which bears in every line the impress of his own personality, which nobody else could have written. It is a real recon-
struction of the life of its period as Browning saw it, not as he
believed Shakespeare or Webster would have seen it. It has its
alternation of blank verse and homely prose, but here too Browning
is no mere imitator. He does not simply borrow a trick from the
Elizabethans. His first, second and third citizens talk their prose
and make their simple jokes in it, but their speeches never for a
moment read like a parody of the gravediggers in *Hamlet*. And it
is not only the citizens who talk prose. The Papal Legate talks
prose too—because he thinks prose. So do the romantic characters,
Chiappino and the rest, when they have come down from the romantic heights and have to face a commonplace, practical issue.
Browning himself, it will be remembered, divides the play into two
parts, "Act I, being what was called the poetry of Chiappino's life,
and Act II, its prose," and he writes the first act in verse and the
second in prose to carry out the idea. This is to give a fresh
significance to the traditional blending of verse and prose in
tragedy, and put fresh life into what had become an obsolete convention. If *The Duchess of Padua* had been written with the artistic
sincerity of *A Soul's Tragedy*—Wilde, by the way, admired that play
very highly—Mr. Ross would not have had to write so deprecatingly
of it in his dedicatory letter.

The same imitative quality which prevents one from taking *The
Duchess of Padua* seriously as a work of art mars the comedies also.
As far as plot and construction are concerned they are frankly
modelled on the "well-made play" of their period. Indeed, they were
already old-fashioned in technique when they were written. The
long soliloquy which opens the third act of *Lady Windermere's Fan*
with such appalling staginess, and sends a cold shiver down one's
back at each successive revival, was almost equally out of date on
the first night. Ibsen had already sent that kind of thing to the
right-about for all persons who aspired to serious consideration as
dramatists. Luckily the fame of Wilde's comedies does not rest on his

plots or his construction. It rests on his gifts of characterisation and of brilliant and effective dialogue. Both these gifts he possessed in a pre-eminent degree, but in both of them one has to recognise grave limitations. His minor characters are generally first-rate, but he never quite succeeded with his full-length figures. He is like an artist who can produce marvellously life-like studies or sketches, but fails when he attempts to elaborate a portrait. Windermere and Lady Windermere, Sir Robert and Lady Chiltern, none of them is really human, none of them quite alive. As for the principal people in *A Woman of No Importance*, Lord Illingworth himself, Mrs. Arbuthnot and her son, Hester Worsley, they are all dolls. The sawdust leaks out of them at every pore. That is the central weakness of the play, that and its preposterous plot. But when you turn to the minor characters, to Lady Hunstanton and Lady Caroline Pontefract and Sir John and the Archdeacon, how admirably they are drawn! Did anybody ever draw foolish or pompous or domineering old ladies better than Wilde? Think of Lady Hunstanton's deliciously idiotic reply to poor Miss Worsley when that American young lady, with impassioned fervour, has just been proclaiming to the assembled company the domestic virtues of her countrymen who are "trying to build up something that will last longer than brick or stone." "What is that, dear?" asks Lady Hunstanton with perfect simplicity. "Ah yes, an Iron Exhibition, is it not, at that place which has the curious name?" How it sets before us in a flash the whole character of the speaker, her gentleness, her stupidity, her admirable good breeding as contrasted with Miss Worsley's crude provincialism! Or again, think of that other reply of hers when Mrs. Allonby tells her that in the Hunstanton conservatories there is an orchid that is "as beautiful as the Seven Deadly Sins." "My dear, I hope there is nothing of the kind. I will certainly speak to the gardener."

Lady Caroline is equally well drawn, with her sharp tongue and her shrewd masculine common sense. She also has a brief encounter with Miss Worsley, in which the latter is again put to rout, but by quite different means. Lady Hunstanton conquered by sheer gentle futility. Lady Caroline administers a deliberate snub, all the more crushing because it is given with a deadly semblance of unconsciousness. Here is the scene:

Hester. Lord Henry Weston! I remember him, Lady Hunstanton. A man with a hideous smile and a hideous past. He is asked everywhere. No dinner-party is complete without him. What of those whose ruin is due to him? They are outcasts. They are nameless. If you met them in the street you would turn your head away. I don't complain of their punishment. Let all women who have sinned be punished.

Lady Hunstanton. My dear young lady!

Hester. It is right that they should be punished, but don't let them be the only ones to suffer. If a man and a woman have sinned, let them both go forth into the desert to love or loathe each other there. Let them both be branded. Set a mark, if you wish, on each, but don't punish the one and let the other go free. Don't have one law for men and another for women. You are unjust to women in England. And till you count what is a shame in a woman to be an infamy in a man, you will always be unjust, and Right, that pillar of fire, and Wrong, that pillar of cloud, will be made dim to your eyes, or be not seen at all, or if seen, not regarded.

Lady Caroline. Might I, dear Miss Worsley, as you are standing up, ask you for my cotton that is just behind you? Thank you.

It must be admitted that in order to get this effect, Wilde has exaggerated the rhetoric of Miss Worsley's speech to an unfair degree, thereby "loading the dice" against her in the encounter. But the effect is so admirable in the theatre that one forgives the means.

When I say that it was only in his "minor characters" that Wilde was completely successful, I do not mean unimportant characters, or characters who only make brief appearances in his plays, such as the walking ladies and gentlemen in his evening parties, or the impassive men-servants who wait upon Lord Goring and Mr. Algernon Moncrieff. I include under the description all the people who are not emotionally of prime importance to the plot. Lady Bracknell and the Duchess of Berwick are very important parts in the plays in which they appear, and Wilde obviously took an immense amount of trouble with them, but they are not emotionally important as Lady Windermere is or Mrs. Erlynne. In that sense they are minor characters. It is in the drawing of such characters that Wilde is seen absolutely at his best. Who can ever forget Lady Bracknell's superb scene with Mr. Worthing in *The Importance of Being Earnest,* when she puts that gentleman through a series of questions as he is "not on her list of eligible bachelors, though she has the same list as the dear Duchess of Bolton"? Who can forget the inimitable speech in which she sums up the sorrows of the modern landowner?

"What between the duties expected of one during one's lifetime, and the duties exacted from one after one's death, land has ceased to be either a profit or a pleasure. It gives one position, and prevents one from keeping it up. That is all that can be said about land."

Yes, Lady Bracknell is an immortal creation. She is in some ways the greatest achievement of the Wilde theatre, the fine flower of his genius. It is impossible to read any of her scenes—indeed, it is impossible to read almost any scene whatever in *The Importance of Being Earnest*—without recognising that for brilliancy of wit this play may fairly be ranked with the very greatest of English comedies. But though Lady Bracknell is wonderfully drawn, she is not profoundly drawn. As a character in so very light a comedy, there is, of course, no reason why she should be. I merely mention the fact lest she should be claimed as an exception to the statement that Wilde's more elaborate portraits are all failures. Lady Bracknell is brilliantly done, but she is a brilliant surface only. She has no depth and no subtlety. Wilde has seen her with absolute clearness, but he has seen her, as it were, in two dimensions only, not in the round. That is the weak point of all Wilde's character drawing. It lacks solidity. No one can hit off people's external manifestations, their whims and mannerisms, their social insincerities, more vividly or more agreeably than he. But he never shows you their souls. And when it is necessary that he should do so, if you are really to understand and to sympathise with them, as it is in the case of Mrs. Arbuthnot, for example, or Lady Chiltern, he fails.

Why he failed I do not know. Possibly it was from mere indolence, because he was not sufficiently interested. Possibly he could not have succeeded if he had tried. To analyse character to the depths requires imaginative sympathy of a very special kind, and I am not sure whether Wilde possessed this, or at least possessed it in the requisite degree of intensity. He had a quick eye for the foibles of mankind and a rough working hypothesis as to their passions and weaknesses. Beyond that he does not seem to me to have gone, and I doubt whether it ever occurred to him to examine the springs of

action of even his most important characters with any thorough-
ness. So long as what they did and the reasons assigned for their
doing it would pass muster in the average English theatre with the
average English audience, he was content. That is not the spirit in
which the great characters of dramatic literature have been conceived.

The fact is, Wilde despised the theatre. He was a born dramatist
in the sense that he was naturally equipped with certain very
valuable gifts for writing for the stage. But he was not a dramatist
from conviction in the sense that Ibsen was or that Mr. Shaw is.
Ibsen wrote plays, not because play-writing seemed a particularly
promising or remunerative calling in the Norway of his day. It did
not. He wrote plays because the dramatic form irresistibly attracted
him. Mr. Shaw writes plays because he believes in the stage as an
influence, as the most powerful and the most far-reaching of pulpits.
Wilde's attitude towards the theatre was utterly different from either
of these. He wrote plays frankly for the market and because play-
writing was lucrative. Of course, he put a certain amount of himself
into them. No artist can help doing that. But no artist of Wilde's
power and originality ever did it less. His plays were frankly manu-
factured to meet a demand and to earn money. There is, of course,
no reason why an artist should not work for money. Indeed, all
artists do so more or less. They have to live like their neighbours.
Unhappily, Wilde wanted a great deal of money, and he wanted
it quickly. He loved luxury, and luxury cannot be had for nothing.
And if an artist wants a large income and wants it at once, he generally has to condescend a good deal to get it. Wilde condescended.
He looked around him at the kind of stuff which other playwrights
were making money by, examined it with contemptuous acumen,
saw how it was done—and went and did likewise. The only one of
his plays which seems to me to be written with conviction, because
he had something to express and because the dramatic form seemed
to him the right one in which to express it, is *Salome*—and *Salome*
was not written for the theatre. When Wilde wrote it he had no idea
of its ever being acted. But when Madame Bernhardt one day asked
him in jest why he had never written her a play, he replied, equally
in jest, "I have," and sent her *Salome*. She read it, and, as we know,
would have produced it in London if the Censor of Plays had not

intervened. But when Wilde wrote it, it was not with a view to its ever being performed, and so his genius had free scope. He was writing to please himself, not to please a manager, and the result is that *Salome* is his best play. *The Importance of Being Earnest* is written with conviction, in a sense. That is to say, it is the expression of the author's own temperament and his attitude towards life, not an insincere re-statement of conventional theatrical ideas. But *The Importance of Being Earnest* is only a joke, though an amazingly brilliant one, and Wilde seems to have looked upon it with the same amused contempt with which he looked on its predecessors. Perhaps he did not realise how good it was. At least he treated it with scant respect, for the original script was in four acts, and these were boiled down into three and the loose ends joined up in perfunctory fashion for purposes of representation. I wonder whether there is any copy of that four-act version still in existence, by the way? It is just possible that a copy is to be found at the Lord Chamberlain's office, for it may have been submitted for license in its original form. If so, I hope Mr. Ross will obtain permission to copy it with a view to its publication. If the deleted act is half as delightful as the three that survive, every playgoer will long to read it. But that a man of Wilde's theatrical skill and experience should have written a play which required this drastic "cutting"—or should have allowed it to be so cut if it did not require it—is an eloquent proof of his contempt for play-writing as an art.

Yes, Wilde despised the drama, and the drama avenged itself. With his gifts for dialogue and characterisation, his very remarkable "sense of the theatre," he might have been a great dramatist if he had been willing to take his art seriously. But he was not willing. The result was that in the age of Ibsen and of Hauptmann, of Strindberg and Brieux, he was content to construct like Sardou and think like Dumas *fils*. Had there been a National Theatre in this country in his day, or any theatre of dignity and influence to which a dramatist might look to produce plays for their artistic value, not solely for their value in the box office, Wilde might, I believe, have done really fine work for it. But there was not. And Wilde loved glitter and success. It would not have amused him to write "uncommercial" masterpieces to be produced for half a dozen *matinées* at a Boxers' Hall. His ambition—if he can be said to have had any "ambition" at all where the theatre was concerned—did not lie in that direction. So he took the stage as he found it, and wrote "pot-boilers." It is not the least of the crimes of the English theatre of the end of the nineteenth century that it could find nothing to do with a fine talent such as Wilde's save to degrade and waste it.

Overtures to *Salome*

by *Richard Ellmann*

Salome, after having danced before the imaginations of European painters and sculptors for a thousand years, in the nineteenth
century turned her beguilements to literature. Heine, Flaubert,
Mallarmé, Huysmans, Laforgue and Wilde became her suitors.
Jaded by exaltations of nature and of humanism, they inspected
with something like relief a Biblical image of the *un*natural. Mario
Praz, bluff, and skeptical of Salome's allurements, seeks to limit them
by arguing that she became the type of no more than the *femme
fatale*. By type he means, he says, something "like a neuralgic area.
Some chronic ailment has created a zone of weakened resistance,
and whenever an analogous phenomenon makes itself felt, it immediately confines itself to this predisposed area, until the process
becomes a matter of mechanical monotony." [1] But like most medical
metaphors, this one doesn't apply easily to the arts, where repetition
of subject is not a certain contra-indication to achievement. Most
of these writers were conspicuous for their originality, and if they
embraced so familiar a character from Biblical history, it was to
accomplish effects they intended to make distinctive. As there are
many Iseults, many Marys, so there were many Salomes, without
monotony.

The fact that Wilde's *Salome* is a play, and a completed one, distinguishes it from other versions and helps to make it more original
than Mr. Praz would have us believe. Mallarmé was not merely flat-
tering when he congratulated Wilde on the "definitive evocation"

"Overtures to *Salome*" by Richard Ellmann. From *Yearbook of Comparative
and General Literature*, No. 17 (1968), 17–28; and *Tri-Quarterly*. Copyright ©
1968 by *Yearbook of Comparative and General Literature* and © 1968 by *Tri-
Quarterly* for the revisions made in the original article. Reprinted by permission.

[1] Mario Praz, *The Romantic Agony*, tr. Angus Davidson (Meridian Books,
1963), p. 191.

of Salome,[2] or when he took care to avoid seeming to copy Wilde when he returned to work on his own *Hérodiade*.[3] Wilde's simple sentences and repeated words may indeed owe something to Maeterlinck or even (as a contemporary critic suggested) to Ollendorff—the Berlitz of that age—but they have become so habitual in modern drama as to seem anticipatory rather than derivative. The extreme concentration upon a single episode which is like an image, with a synchronized moon changing color from pale to blood-red in keeping with the action, and an atmosphere of frenzy framed in exotic chill, confirms Yeats's oblique acknowledgement that he had learned as much from Wilde as from the Noh drama for his dance plays.[4] A torpid tetrarch (three Herods telescoped into one) lusting yet inert, a prophet clamoring from a well below the floorboards, are more congenial figures now that Beckett has accustomed us to paralysis, senile drivelling, voices from ashcans, and general thwart.

Mr. Praz, quick to deny Wilde any novelty, insists that the play's culminating moment, when Salome kisses the severed head of Iokanaan, is borrowed from Heine's *Atta Troll*.[5] But in Heine's version kissing the head is a punishment after Herodias's death, not a *divertissement* before it, and the tone of caricature is quite unlike that of perverted horror which Wilde evokes. If some source has to be found —and it always has—I offer tentatively a dramatic poem called *Salome* published in Cambridge, Massachusetts, in 1862, by a young Harvard graduate named J. C. Heywood,[6] and subsequently republished during the 1880s in London in the form of a trilogy. I have to admit that in Heywood as in Heine, it is Herodias, not Salome, who kisses the head, but at least she does so while still alive, and in a sufficiently grisly way. Wilde knew one part of Heywood's trilogy —he reviewed it in 1888, three years before writing his own play[7]—

---

[2] ". . . cette jeune princesse que définitivement vous évoquâtes." Unpublished letter, Mallarmé to Wilde, March 1893.

[3] "J'ai laissé le nom d'Hérodiade pour bien la différencier de la Salome je dirai moderne . . ." Draft of a preface to *Hérodiade*, in Stéphane Mallarmé, *Les Noces d'Hérodiade* (Paris, 1959), p. 51.

[4] See Yeats's comments on *A Full Moon in March* and *The King of the Great Clock Tower*.

[5] Praz, p. 299.

[6] This edition was anonymous.

[7] Heywood's *Salome* was one of several books discussed in Wilde's review, "The Poet's Corner," *Pall Mall Gazette*, XLVII:7128 (January 20, 1888), 3.

and he may well have glanced at the other parts. Still, he isn't really
dependent on Heywood either, since he exchanges mother for
daughter and, unlike Heywood, makes this monstrous kissing the
play's climax.[8]

To read Heywood or other writers about Salome is to come to a
greater admiration for Wilde's ingenuity. The general problem that
I want to inquire into is what the play probably meant to Wilde and
how he came to write it. Villainous women were not his usual subject, and even if they had been, there were others besides Salome he
could have chosen. The reservoir of villainous women is always
brimming. The choice of Salome would seem to inhere in her spe-⌉
cial relationship to John the Baptist and Herod. Sources offer little
help in understanding this, and we have to turn to what might be
called praeter-sources, elements which so pervaded Wilde's imaginative life as to become presences. Such a presence Amadis was for
Don Quixote, or Vergil for Dante. In pursuing these I will offer no
explication de texte, but what may well appear a divagation; perhaps to give it critical standing I should pronounce it *divagation,*
though I hope to persuade you of its clandestine relevance. It includes, at any rate, those fugitive associations, often subliminal,
which swarm beneath the fixed surface of the work, and which are
as pertinent as is that surface to any study of the author's mind.   ⌋

It will be necessary, therefore, to retrace certain of Wilde's close
relationships. If Rilke is right in finding a few moments in a writer's
life to be initiatory, then such an initiatory experience took place
when Wilde left Ireland for England. He later said that the two
turning-points in his life occurred "when my father sent me to Oxford, and when society sent me to prison." [9] Wilde matriculated at
Magdalen College, Oxford, on October 11, 1874, just before he was
twenty. The two men he had most wanted to know at that time, he
said, were Ruskin and Pater,[10] both, conveniently enough, installed ⟨
at the same place. He managed to meet Ruskin within a month, and ⟨
though he didn't meet Pater so quickly, during his first three months

[8] According to E. Gomez Carrillo, a young Guatemalan writer who saw much
of Wilde during the composition of the play, other details changed considerably
in the planning, but the climax was always the same. E. Gomez Carrillo, *En
Plena Bohemia,* in Collected Works (Madrid, n.d. [1919?]), xvi, 190ff.

[9] Oscar Wilde, *Letters,* ed. Rupert Hart-Davis (London, 1962), p. 469.

[10] Vincent O'Sullivan, *Aspects of Wilde* (London, 1936), p. 139.

at Oxford he made the acquaintance of Pater's *Studies in the History of the Renaissance*,[11] which he soon called his "golden book," [12] and subsequently referred to in a portentous phrase as "that book which has had such a strange influence over my life." [13]

Three weeks after Wilde arrived, Ruskin gave a series of lectures on Florentine painting. During one of them he proposed to his students that, instead of developing their bodies in pointless games, in learning "to leap and to row, to hit a ball with a bat," [14] they join him in improving the countryside. He proposed to turn a swampy lane near Ferry Hincksey into a flower-bordered country road. Such muscular effort would be ethical rather than narcissistic, medieval rather than classical.[15] Although Oscar Wilde found rising at dawn more difficult than most men, he overcame his languor for Ruskin's sake. He would later brag comically that he had had the distinction of being allowed to fill "Mr. Ruskin's especial wheelbarrow" and even of being instructed by the master himself in the mysteries of wheeling such an object from place to place. At the end of term Ruskin was off to Venice, and Wilde could again lie late abed, comfortable in the thought that, as he said, "there was a long mound of earth across that swamp which a lively imagination might fancy was a road." [16] The merely external signs of this noble enterprise soon sank from sight, but Wilde remembered it with affectionate respect, and his later insistence on functionalism in decoration and in women's dress, and on socialism based upon self-fulfillment in groups, were in the Ferry Hincksey tradition.

The road proved also to be the road to Ruskin. Wilde met his exalted foreman often during the ensuing years. In 1888, sending him a book, he summed up his feelings in this effusive tribute: "The dearest memories of my Oxford days are my walks and talks with you, and from you I learned nothing but what was good. How else could it be? There is in you something of prophet, of priest, and

[11] Wilde, *Letters*, p. 471.

[12] Yeats, *Autobiography* (New York, 1965), p. 87.

[13] Wilde, *Letters*, p. 471. At the Lord Queensberry trial Wilde spoke of Pater as "the only critic of the century whose opinion I set high. . . ."

[14] John Ruskin, *Sesame and Lilies* (London, 1900), p. 203.

[15] Pater, on the other hand, much preferred the activities of what he called in italics the palaestra.

[16] Based on newspaper clippings of Wilde's American tour, 1881–82.

of poet, and to you the gods gave eloquence such as they have given
to none other, so that your message might come to us with the fire
of passion, and the marvel of music, making the deaf to hear, and
the blind to see." [17] That (like this prose) the prophet had weaknesses, made him if anything more prophetlike. Wilde was as aware
of Ruskin's weaknesses as of his virtues. His letter of November 28,
1879, by which time he had taken his Oxford degree, mentions that
he and Ruskin were going that night to see Henry Irving play
Shylock, following which he himself was going on to the Millais
ball. "How odd it is," Wilde remarks.[18] The oddity lay not only in
attending this particular play with the author of *The Stones of
Venice*, but in proceeding afterwards to a ball which celebrated the
marriage of John Everett Millais's daughter. Mrs. Millais had for
six years been Mrs. Ruskin, and for three of those years Millais had
been Ruskin's friend and protegé. The details of Ruskin's marriage
and annulment were no doubt as well known at that time at Oxford
by word of mouth as they have since become to us by dint of a dozen
books. It was the fact that Ruskin and the Millaises did not speak
to each other that obliged Wilde to leave Ruskin with Irving and
proceed to the ball alone.

To call the Ruskin ambiance merely odd was Oxonian politeness.
As soon as Ruskin was married, he explained to his wife that children would interfere with his work and impede necessary scholarly
travel. Consummation might therefore wisely be deferred until later
on, perhaps in six years' time when Effie would be twenty-five. Few
of us here could claim an equal dedication to learning. In the
meantime Effie need have no fear about the possible sinfulness of
their restraint, since many early Christians lived in married celibacy
all their lives. Effie tried to accommodate herself to this pedantic
view, and Ruskin in turn was glad to oblige her on a lesser matter:
that they go to live in Venice, since he was already planning to write
a book about that city.

In Venice, while Ruskin sketched, Effie survived her boredom by
going about with one or another of their friends. Ruskin encouraged her, perhaps (as she afterwards implied) too much. If he ac-
companied her to dances and masked balls, he often left early with-

[17] Wilde, *Letters,* p. 218.
[18] *Ibid.,* p. 61.

out her, having arranged that some gentleman friend escort her home. If she returned at 1:30 in the morning, he duly notified his parents in England, at the same time adding that he was completely at rest about her fidelity.[19] Yet her obvious pleasure in pleasure, her flirtatiousness, her impatience with his studies, her delight in frivolity and late hours, struck Ruskin sometimes—however much he repudiated the outward thought—as forms of misconduct and disloyalty. He said as much later. That Effie wasn't sexually unfaithful to him didn't of course prevent Ruskin, any more than it prevented Othello before him, from considering her so, or from transposing her mental dissonance into larger, vaguer forms of betrayal.

The Stones of Venice will always stand primarily as a work of art criticism. But criticism, as Wilde said, is the only civilized form of autobiography,[20] and it is as a fragment—a large fragment—of Ruskin's autobiography that the book claims an added interest. In novels and poems we take for granted that some personal elements will be reflected, but in works of non-fiction we are more reluctant, and prefer to postulate an upper air of abstraction in which the dispassionate mind contemplates and orders materials that already have form and substance. Yet even the most impersonal of writers, Thucydides, writing about the fortunes of another city, shaped his events, as Cornford suggests, by preconceptions absorbed from Greek tragedy. Ruskin made no pretense of Thucydidean impersonality, and the influence of his reading of the Bible is manifest rather than latent. But some problems of his own life also were projected onto the Venetian scene. Rather than diminishing the book's value, they merge with its talent and add to its intensity.

It may be easier to be convinced that *The Stones of Venice* is in part autobiographical if we remember Ruskin's candid admission that *Sesame and Lilies*, a book he wrote a few years later, was a reflection of one particular experience. His preface expressly states that the section in it called "Lilies" was generated by his love for Rose La Touche. This love impelled him to idealize women, he says, even though "the chances of later life gave me opportunities of watching women in states of degradation and vindictiveness which opened to me the gloomiest secrets of Greek and Syrian tragedy. I

[19] Derrick Leon, *Ruskin, The Great Victorian* (London, 1949), p. 152.
[20] In *The Critic as Artist*.

have seen them betray their household charities to lust, their pledged love to devotion; I have seen mothers dutiful to their children, as Medea; and children dutiful to their parents, as the daughter of Herodias. . . ." His love for Rose La Touche also covertly leads him to quarrel in the book with pietism because Rose was that way inclined. *The Stones of Venice* deals less obviously, but with the same insistence, on the virtues and defects of the feminine character. As Ruskin remarks in *Sesame and Lilies*, "it has chanced to me, untowardly in some respects, fortunately in others *(because it enables me to read history more clearly)*,[21] to see the utmost evil that is in women. . . ." [22] To Ruskin Venice is always *she* (to Mary McCarthy, invariably *it*), and the gender is not merely a form of speech but an image to be enforced in detail.

Accordingly Ruskin distinguishes two stages, with medieval Venice as virgin and Renaissance Venice as whore. The moment of transition is, apparently, the moment of copulation, and the moment of copulation is therefore (as in a familiar view of the Garden of Eden) the fall. When Ruskin describes the fallen state, he attributes to the city the very taste for masqued balls and merriment which he had ostentatiously tolerated in his wife. "She became in after times," he declares, "the revel of the earth, the masque of Italy: and *therefore* is she now desolate, but her glorious robe of gold and purple was given her when first she rose a vestal from the sea, not when she became drunk with the wine of her fornication." [23] At the end of the first volume he again asserts, "It was when she wore the ephod of the priest, not the motley of the masquer, that the fire fell upon her from heaven. . . ." [24] After that fire came another which changed the virgin city to its contrary: "Now Venice, as she was once the most religious, was in her fall the most corrupt, of European states; and as she was in her strength the centre of the pure currents of Christian architecture, so she is in her decline the source of the Renaissance. It was the originality and splendour of the Palaces of Vicenza and Venice which gave this school its eminence in the eyes of Europe; and the dying city, magnificent in her dissipation, and graceful in her follies, obtained wider worship in

[21] My italics.
[22] *Sesame and Lilies,* p. xxxiii.
[23] Ruskin, *The Stones of Venice* (New York, n.d.), I, 150.
[24] *Ibid.,* p. 8.

her decrepitude than in her youth, and sank from the midst of her admirers into her grave." [25] Ruskin cannot bring himself to sketch out "the steps of her final ruin. That ancient curse was upon her, the curse of the cities of the plain, 'pride, fulness of bread, and abundance of idleness.' By the inner burning of her own passions, as fatal as the fiery reign of Gomorrah, she was consumed from her place among the nations, and her ashes are choking the channels of the dead salt sea." [26] Just how passions should burn except inwardly may not be clear, especially since we can't suppose that Ruskin favored the translation of sensual thought into sensual action, but pride, gluttony, and sloth secure a more sinister confederate in the unnamable sin of lust, whose self-generated fire is contrasted with that fire which had earlier fallen on the city from heaven.

Ruskin's stridency shows how much he had this problem at heart. In fact, consummation and defilement were irrevocably united for him, in his life as in his criticism. The Renaissance (a new term then but already favorable in its connotations)[27] was for him not a re-birth but a relapse. (In *De Profundis* Wilde accepted this view.) Ruskin's revulsion extended from coupling to begetting to having been begot. He had more trouble than most people in allowing that he was himself the product of his parents' intercourse. A small indi-cation is to be found in an epitaph which he wrote for his mother (who already had an epitaph) long after her death, consecrating a memorial well, as he writes, "in memory of a maid's life as pure, and a mother's love as ceaseless. . . ." [28] In Ruskin's mind his

---

[25] *Ibid.*, pp. 38–39.

[26] *Ibid.*, III, 165.

[27] Wallace K. Ferguson, *The Renaissance in Historical Thought* (Cambridge, Massachusetts, 1948), pp. 142–4.

[28] Entry for 30 November 1880, in *The Diaries of John Ruskin*, ed. Joan Evans and John Howard Whitehouse (Oxford, 1959), III, 995. Ruskin's earlier dedica-tory tablet had been taken down because the well became polluted. It specified that the name 'Margaret's Well' be given, but did not otherwise mention his mother, though the donor's name was given as "John Ruskin Esq., M.A., LL.D." The new inscription, never installed, was to read in full:

"This Spring
In memory of a maid's life as pure
And a mother's love as ceaseless,
Dedicate to a spirit in peace
Is called by Croydon people,
Margaret's Well.
Matris animae, Joannes Ruskin
1880"

mother had immaculately passed from maid to mother without ever becoming a wife.

This singular epitaph may illuminate a point never adequately explained, why Ruskin dated the fall of Venice not only to an exact year, but to a specific day, May 8, 1418.[29] His own explanation is that this was the deathday of the aged Venetian military leader Carlo Zeno, and he makes his usual citation of Pierre Daru's *Histoire de la République de Venise* as his authority. But Daru doesn't give Zeno's death such consequence.[30] Ruskin might more easily, and more consistently with his own views, have taken the year 1423, when the old Doge Tommaso Mocenigo died and the new Doge, Foscari, began his less glorious rule. He is alone among writers on Venice in attaching this significance to Zeno's deathday, and in view of his known penchant for numerology the date invites attention. If Ruskin had been born exactly four hundred years after this date, in 1818, rather than in 1819, the choice might seem related to his theatrical self-laceration, as if to regret he had ever been born. But his terrors were for intercourse and conception rather than for birth. At the risk of impugning my own sanity as well as Ruskin's, I venture to propose that the date so carefully selected was, putatively, four hundred years to the day before his own conception— that act so impossible for him to meditate on with equanimity. That the moment of Venice's fall should be reiterated in the moment of his own begetting and be followed by his birth into an England only too ready (as he announces on the first page of his book) to fall —like a semi-detached Venice—anchored firmly the relationships Ruskin wished to dwell upon. In his parents' fall, as in that of our first parents, he saw the determination of an age's character and of his own.

Margaret Ruskin's marriage had made her a mother, while Effie Ruskin's "dissolute" behavior in Venice had made her—in fancy if not in fact—an adultress. Moral blame, from which his mother was freed, was shunted to his wife. Ruskin's own later summary of *The Stones of Venice* confirms that he had this theme in mind. In *The Crown of Wild Olive* (1866) he wrote, "*The Stones of Venice* had, from beginning to end, no other aim than to show that the Renaissance architecture of Venice had arisen out of, and in all its features

[29] *The Stones of Venice*, I, 18.
[30] Pierre Daru, *Histoire de la République de Venise* (Paris, 1853), II, 198–9.

indicated, a state of concealed national infidelity, and of domestic corruption."[31] The trip to Scotland which Ruskin, his wife, and Millais took in 1853 strengthened the metaphors, and in later life he accused Millais of infidelity—artistic infidelity he called it[32]—to the Pre-Raphaelite principles as Ruskin had earlier enunciated them. Venice, his wife, and his friend were all guilty of the same crime.

Necessary as Ruskin found it to think of himself as wronged, there were moments when he recognized his own culpability. After the annulment of his marriage he came, by a series of mental leaps, to try a revision of his character. In 1858, while looking at Veronese's "Solomon and Sheba" in Turin, he suddenly felt a wave of sympathy for the "strong and frank animality" of the greatest artists.[33] He disavowed his earlier religious zeal, and became (though at the urging of his father and of Rose La Touche's mother he didn't publicly say so) quite skeptical. Then, as Wilenski points out, he began to acknowledge that his theory of history in *The Stones of Venice* was mistaken. Writing to Froude in 1864, he stated firmly, "There is no law of history any more than of a kaleidoscope. With certain bits of glass—shaken so, and so—you will get pretty figures, but what figures, Heaven only knows. . . . The wards of a Chubb's lock are infinite in their chances. Is the Key of Destiny made on a less complex principle?"[34] This renunciation of historical law was intellectually daring, and emotionally as well, for it meant that he was trying to alter those "pretty figures" which earlier had enabled him to lock his own conception and marriage into the history of Venice. As part of this change, he resolved to propose marriage to Rose La Touche, and in 1866 he at last did so.[35] Rose La Touche,

---

[31] Ruskin, *The Crown of Wild Olive* (1866), in *The Works of John Ruskin*, ed. E. T. Cook and Alexander Wedderburn (London, 1903), XVIII, 443.

[32] "But the spectator may still gather from them some conception of what this great painter might have done, had he remained faithful to the principles of his school when he first led its onset." *Fors Clavigera* 79 (July 1877), in *Works*, XXIX, 161.

[33] Ruskin, *Diary*, II, 537, and Notes on the Turin Gallery. Quoted by R. H. Wilenski, *John Ruskin* (London, 1933), pp. 231-2.

[34] Wilenski, p. 69.

[35] The day he selected for the proposal was probably an effort to change his temperament as well as his luck by another numerological flurry, for it was February 2, his parents' wedding day. By this symbolism he planned, perhaps, to overcome his revulsion at the thought of both consummation and procreation.

no mean calendar-watcher herself, said she could not answer for two years, or perhaps for four. Ruskin abided by her verdict with desperation; his diary records the passing of not only these anniversaries but, since she died soon after, of year after year following her death.[36] No one will mock Ruskin's pain, or his struggle to overcome his fears and become as animal as Veronese.

Rose La Touche had been dead less than a year when Ruskin and Wilde met and took walks together. Neither professor nor pupil was reticent, and Wilde probably divined the matters that Ruskin was unwilling to confide. At any rate, the moral law as imparted by Ruskin, even with the softenings he now wished to introduce, was for Wilde sublime—and berserk. In Ruskin, whom everyone called a prophet, the ethical life was noble and yet, in its weird chastity, perverse. Against its rigors life offered an antidote, and what life was had been articulated by Pater, who saw it not in terms of stones but of waters, not of monuments but of rivery passions. Pater was like Wilde in that, at the same age of nineteen, he too had fallen under Ruskin's sway. He soon broke free, his conscience unclenched itself. He surprised a devout friend by nonetheless attempting, although he had lost his faith, to take orders in the Anglican Church. His friend complained to the bishop and scotched this diabolic ordination. The *Studies in the History of the Renaissance*, Pater's first book, doesn't mention Ruskin by name, but uses him throughout as an adversary. Pater's view of the Renaissance did not differ in being more detached; in its way it was just as personal, and it ended in a secular sermon which ran exactly counter to that of *The Stones of Venice*. It is Ruskin inverted. Pater is all blend where Ruskin is all severance. He calls superficial Ruskin's view that the Renaissance was "a fashion which set in at a definite period." For Pater it was rather "an uninterrupted effort of the middle age." [37] One age was older, one younger, they encountered each other like lovers.

An atmosphere of suppressed invitation runs through Pater's book as an atmosphere of suppressed refusal runs through Ruskin's. The first essay of *Studies in the . . . Renaissance* recounts at length how the friendship of Amis and Amile (in the thirteenth-century story)

---

[36] *Diary*, II, 720, 737.
[37] Walter Pater, *The Renaissance*, ed. Kenneth Clark (Meridian, 1961), p. 214.

was so full and intense that they were buried together rather than with their respective wives. Later essays dwell with feeling upon such encounters as that of young Pico della Mirandola, looking like a Phidian statue, with the older Ficino, or as that—planned but prevented by murder—of Winckelmann and the still callow Goethe. For Ruskin the Renaissance is an aged Jezebel, while for Pater it is a young man, his hair wreathed in roses more than in thorns, such a youth as Leonardo painted as John the Baptist. In describing this painting, Pater lingers to point out that the saint's body doesn't look as if it had come from a wilderness, and he finds John's smile intriguingly treacherous[38] and suggestive of a good deal [39]—which may be Victorian hinting at the heresy, a specially homosexual one, that Christ and John (not to mention Leonardo and his model) were lovers.[40]

Whatever Ruskin says about strength and weakness, Pater opposes. The decay against which *The Stones of Venice* fulminates is for Pater "the fascination of corruption," [41] and images of baleful female power, such as Leonardo's Medusa and other "daughters of Herodias," are discovered to be "clairvoyant" and "electric," [42] when Ruskin had found the daughter of Herodias monstrously degraded. Instead of praising the principle of *Noli me tangere*, so ardently espoused by Ruskin, Pater objects to Christian asceticism that it "discredits the slightest sense of touch." Ruskin had denounced "ripe" ornamentation in terms which evoked elements of the adult female body: "I mean," he said, "that character of extravagance in the ornament itself which shows that it was addressed to jaded faculties; a violence and coarseness in curvature, a depth of shadow, a lusciousness in arrangement of line, evidently arising out of an incapability of feeling the true beauty of chaste forms and restrained

[38] Wilde wrote from Algiers in 1895 to Robert Ross, "The most beautiful boy in Algiers is said by the guide to be 'deceitful'; isn't it sad? Bosie and I are terribly upset about it." (Unpublished text from Sir Rupert Hart-Davis)

[39] "It is so with the so-called *Saint John the Baptist* of the Louvre—one of the few naked figures Leonardo painted—whose delicate brown flesh and woman's hair no one would go out into the wilderness to seek, and whose treacherous smile would have us understand something far beyond the outward gesture or circumstances." Pater, *Renaissance*, p. 118.

[40] See Wilde, *Letters*, p. 756.

[41] *Ibid.*, p. 108.

[42] *Ibid.*, p. 116.

power. I do not know any character of design which may be more
easily recognized at a glance than this over-lusciousness. . . . We
speak loosely and inaccurately of 'overcharged' ornament, with an
obscure feeling that there is indeed something in visible Form
which is correspondent to Intemperance in moral habits. . . ." [43]
But for Pater overcharged ornament is rather an "overwrought delicacy, almost of wantonness," or "a languid Eastern deliciousness." [44]

Ruskin strenuously combatted what he considered to be a false
fusion of classicism and Christianity in the Renaissance. "It would
have been better," he said, "to have worshipped Diana and Jupiter
at once than have gone through life naming one God, imagining
another, and dreading none." [45] Galleries had no business placing
Aphrodite and the Madonna, a Bacchanal and a Nativity, side by
side.[46] But this juxtaposition was exactly what Pater endorsed. For
him European culture was what he called, following Hegel to some
extent, a synthesis. To countervail Ruskin's diptych of Venice as
virgin of the Adriatic and whore of Babylon, he offered as his Renaissance altarpiece the Mona Lisa of Leonardo. His famous description begins, "The presence that rose beside the waters," and it is
clear that he is summoning up not only Lisa, but Venus rising like
Ruskin's favorite city from the sea. Lisa has, according to this gospel
of Saint Walter, mothered both Mary and Helen, exactly the indis-
criminateness, as well as the fecundity, which Ruskin condemned.
Pater's heroine, as Salvador Dali has implied by giving her a mous-
tache more suited to Pater, is an androgyne: the activities attributed
to her, dealing with foreign merchants and diving in deep seas, seem
more male than female. She blends the sexes, she combines sacred
and profane. Like Saint John, she has about her something of the
Borgias.

Against Ruskin's insistence upon innocence, Pater proffers what
he bathetically terms, in the suppressed and then altered and rein-
stated conclusion to the *Renaissance*, "great experiences." He urges
his readers to seek out high passions, only being sure they are passions; later, only being sure they are high. The Renaissance is for

[43] *The Stones of Venice*, III, 8.
[44] Pater, *Renaissance*, p. 47.
[45] *The Stones of Venice*, III, 109.
[46] *Ibid.*, p. 110.

him the playtime of sensation, even its spiritual aspects being studies in forms of sensation. W. H. Mallock parodied this aspect by having Pater, as the effete "Mr. Rose" in *The New Republic*, lust for a pornographic book. Something of the extraordinary effect of Pater's *Renaissance* comes from its being exercises in the seduction of young men by the wiles of culture. And yet Pater may not have seduced them in any way except stylistically. When Wilde presented Lord Alfred Douglas to him, the flagrancy of the homosexual relationship was probably, as Lawrence Evans suggests, the cause of the rift between Pater and Wilde which then developed.

Pater and Ruskin were for Wilde at first imagined, and then actual figures; then they came to stand heraldically, burning unicorn and uninflamed satyr, in front of two portals of his mental theatre. He sometimes allowed them to battle, at other times tried to reconcile them. A good example is his first long published work. This was an ambitious review of the paintings in a new London gallery; he wrote it in 1877, his third year at Oxford, for the *Dublin University Magazine*. The article takes the form of a rove through the three rooms, which had been done, Wilde said admiringly, "in scarlet damask above a dado of dull green and gold." (Ruskin, who also attended, complained that this décor was "dull in itself" and altogether unsuited to the pictures.) Upon entering, Wilde immediately belauds Burne-Jones and Hunt as "the greatest masters of colour that we have ever had in England, with the single exception of Turner"—a compliment to Ruskin's advocacy of Turner and to the sponsorship of the Pre-Raphaelites by both Ruskin and Pater. Wilde then, to praise Burne-Jones further, quotes Pater's remark that for Botticelli natural things "have a spirit upon them by which they become expressive to the spirit," and as he sweeps through the gallery he finds occasion to savor the same sweet phrase again. He also manages to mention the portrait of Ruskin by Millais, though it was not on exhibition. Reaching the end, he salutes "that revival of culture and love of beauty which in great part owes its birth to Mr. Ruskin, and which Mr. Swinburne and Mr. Pater and Mr. Symons and Mr. Morris and many others are fostering and keeping alive, each in his peculiar fashion." He slipped another quotation from Pater into this final paragraph, but a watchful editor slipped it out again.

Wilde's review of the exhibition is not so interesting as Ruskin's, in *Fors Clavigera* 79, which roused Millais to fury and Whistler to litigation. But it did result in Wilde's finally meeting Pater who, having been sent a copy of the review, invited him to call. Their subsequent friendship afforded Wilde a chance to study the student of the Renaissance. He did not lose his admiration, as we can surmise from the poem "Hélas!" which he wrote a little later. In it he invokes both of his mentors as if they were contrary forces tugging at him. After owning up to frivolity, Wilde says,

> Surely there was a time I might have trod
> The august[47] heights, and from life's dissonance
> Struck one clear chord to reach the ears of God.

The chief reference is to Gothic architecture, celebrated by Ruskin because, though fraught with human imperfection—"life's dissonance"—it reached towards heaven. In the next lines Wilde confesses to having fallen away a little:

> Is that time dead? Lo, with a little rod,
> I did but touch the honey of romance.
> And must I lose a soul's inheritance?

Here he is quoting Jonathan's remark to Saul, "I did but taste a little honey with the end of the rod that was in mine hand, and lo! I must die," which Wilde remembered Pater's having conspicuously quoted and interpreted in the *Renaissance* in his essay on Winckelmann. For Pater Jonathan's remark epitomizes "the artistic life, with its inevitable sensuousness," and is contrasted with Christian asceticism and its antagonism to touch.[48] If the taste for honey is a little decadent, then so much the better. Wilde is less sanguine about this appetite here. But as Jonathan was saved, so Wilde, for all his

---

[47] Later "sunlit."

[48] Pater, *Renaissance,* p. 211. Compare Ruskin, *Diary,* III, 972, for 1 January 1878: "And now, thinking of the mischief done to my own life and to how many hundred thousand, by dark desire, I open my first text at I Corinthians Vii.1. ['It is good for a man not to touch a woman. Nevertheless . . . let every man have his own wife, and let every woman have her own husband.'] And yet the second verse directly reverses the nobleness of all youthful thought, expressed in a word by Dr. King: 'Not to marry that they may be pure; but to be pure that they may marry.'"

alases, expected to be saved too, partly because he had never renounced the Ruskin conscience, only foregone it for a time.

The tutelary presences of Pater and Ruskin survived in Wilde's
more mature writings. In *The Picture of Dorian Gray*, for example,
Pater is enclosed (like an unhappy dryad caught in a tree trunk) in
Lord Henry Wotton. Lord Henry's chief sin is quoting without
acknowledgment from the *Renaissance*. He tells Dorian, as Pater
told Mona Lisa, "You have drunk deeply of everything . . . and it
has all been to you no more than the sound of music." He predicts,
against the "curious revival of Puritanism" (a cut at Ruskin) a new
hedonism, the aim of which will be "experience itself, and not the
fruits of experience." It will "teach man to concentrate himself upon
the moments of a life that is but a moment." These are obvious tags
from the Conclusion to the *Renaissance*. Lord Henry's advice to
Dorian, "Let nothing be lost upon you. Be always searching for new
sensations," was so closely borrowed from the same essay that Pater,
who wrote a review of the book, was at great pains to distinguish
Lord Henry's philosophy from his own. Wilde seems to have intended not to distinguish them, however, and to offer (through the
disastrous effects of Lord Henry's influence upon Dorian) a criticism
of Pater.

As for Ruskin, his presence in the book is more tangential. The
painter Hallward has little of Ruskin at the beginning, but gradu-
ally he moves closer to that pillar of esthetic taste and moral judgment upon which Wilde leaned, and after Hallward is safely murdered, Dorian with sudden fondness recollects a trip they had made
to Venice together, when his friend was captivated by Tintoretto's
art. Ruskin was of course the English discoverer and champion of
Tintoretto, so that the allusion is specific. The ending of *Dorian
Gray* executes a Ruskinesque repudiation of a Pateresque career of
self-gratifying sensations. Wilde defined the moral in so witty a way
as to content neither of his mentors: in letters to newspapers he said
Dorian Gray showed that "all excess, as well as all renunciation,
brings its own punishment." [49] Not only are Hallward and Dorian
punished by death, but, Wilde asserted, Lord Henry is punished
too. Lord Henry's offense was in seeking "to be merely the spectator

[49] Wilde, letter to the Editor of the *St. James's Gazette,* June 26, 1890, in
Hart-Davis, *Letters of Wilde,* 259.

of life. He finds that those who reject the battle are more deeply wounded than those who take part in it." [50] The phrase "spectator of life" was one that Wilde used in objecting to Pater's *Marius the Epicurean*.[51] However incongruous his conception of himself as activist, with it he lorded it over his too donnish friend. For Pater, while he touted (sporadically at least) the life of pleasure, was careful not to be caught living it. He idealized touch until it became contemplation. He allowed only his eye to participate in the high passions about which he loved to expatiate. Dorian at least had the courage to risk himself.

In *Dorian Gray* the Pater side of Wilde's thought is routed, though not deprived of fascination. Yet Hallward, when his ethical insistence brings him close to Ruskin, is killed too. In *The Soul of Man under Socialism*, also written in 1891, Wilde superimposes Ruskin's social ethic upon Pater's "full expression of personality," fusing instead of destroying them. In *Salome,* to which I come at last, the formulation is close to *Dorian Gray*, with both opposites executed. Behind the figure of Iokanaan lurks the image of that perversely untouching, untouchable prophet John whom Wilde knew at Oxford. When Iokanaan, up from his cistern for a moment, cries to Salome, "Arrière, fille de Sodome! Ne me touchez pas. Il ne faut pas profaner le temple du Seigneur Dieu," a thought of Ruskin, by now sunk down into madness, can scarcely have failed to cross Wilde's mind. By this time Wilde would also have recognized in the prophet's behavior (as in Ruskin's) something of his own, for after his first three years of marriage he had discontinued sexual relations with his wife. Iokanaan is not Ruskin, but he is Ruskinism as Wilde understood that pole of his character. Then when Salome evinces her appetite for strange experiences, her eagerness to kiss a literally disembodied lover in a relation at once totally sensual and totally "mystical" [52] (Wilde's own term for her), she shows something of that diseased contemplation for which Wilde had reprehended Pater. Her adaptation, or perversion, of the Song of Songs to describe a man's rather than a woman's beauty also is reminiscent of

[50] *Ibid.*
[51] Wilde, *Letters*, p. 476.
[52] Jean Paul Raymond and Charles Ricketts, *Oscar Wilde: Recollections* (London, 1932), p. 51.

Pater's *Renaissance* as well as of Wilde's predisposition. It is Salome, and not Pater, who dances the dance of the seven veils, but her virginal yet perverse sensuality is related to Paterism.

Admittedly the play takes place in Judea and not in Oxford. Wilde wanted the play to have meaning outside his own psychodrama. Yet Wilde's tutelary voices from the university, now fully identified as forces within himself, seem to be in attendance, clamoring for domination. Both Iokanaan and Salome are executed, however, and at the command of the tetrarch. The execution of Salome was not in the Bible, but Wilde insisted upon it.[53] So at the play's end the emphasis shifts suddenly to Herod, who is seen to have yielded to Salome's sensuality, and then to the moral revulsion of Iokanaan from that sensuality, and to have survived them both. In Herod Wilde was suggesting that *tertium quid* which he felt to be his own nature, susceptible to contrary impulses but not abandoned for long to either.

Aubrey Beardsley divined the autobiographical element in Herod, and in one of his illustrations gave the tetrarch the author's face. Herod speaks like Wilde in purple passages about peacocks or in such an epigram as, "Il ne faut pas regarder que dans les miroirs. Car les miroirs ne nous montrent que les masques." Just what Wilde thought his own character to be, as distinct from the alternating forces of Pater and Ruskin, is implied in a remark he made in 1883 to George Woodberry, who promptly relayed it to Charles Eliot Norton. Wilde told Woodberry that Ruskin "like Christ bears the sins of the world, but that he himself was 'always like Pilate, washing his hands of all responsibility.' "[54] Pilate in the story of Christ occupies much the same role as Herod in the story of John the Baptist. In other letters Wilde continues to lament his own weakness, yet with so much attention as to imply that it may have a certain fibre to it. In March 1877 he wrote, "I shift with every breath of thought and am weaker and more self-deceiving than ever,"[55] and in 1886 he remarked, "Sometimes I think that the artistic life

[53] Gomez Carrillo says that the play was originally to be entitled "La Décapitation de Salome," thus slighting St. John by precisely equating the two deaths. Gomez Carillo, p. 214.

[54] Unpublished letter in the Houghton Library, Harvard.

[55] Wilde, *Letters*, p. 31.

is a long and lovely suicide, and am not sorry that it is so." [56] What
he more and more held against both his mentors was a vice they
shared equally, that of narrowness. To keep to any one form of life
is limiting, he said in *De Profundis*, and added without remorse,
"I had to pass on." [57]

Herod too passes on, strong in his tremblings, a leaf but a sinuous
one, swept but not destroyed by successive waves of spiritual and
physical passion, in possession of what Wilde in a letter calls "a
curious mixture of ardour and of indifference. I myself would sacrifice everything for a new experience, and I know there is no such
thing as a new experience at all . . . I would go to the stake for a
sensation and be a sceptic to the last!" [58] Here too there are martyrdom and abandonment, with a legal right to choose and yet stay
aloof. Proust had something of the same idea when he said of
Whistler's quarrel with Ruskin that both men were right.[59] In that
same reconciling vein Wilde in *De Profundis* celebrates Christ as an
artist, and the artist as Christ. And in Wilde's last play, when Jack
declares at the end, "I've now realized for the first time in my life
the vital Importance of Being Earnest," he is demonstrating again
that Ruskin's earnestness, and Pater's paraded passionateness, are
for the artist not mutually exclusive but may, by wit, by weakness,
by self-withholding, be artistically, as well as tetrarchically, com-
pounded.

[56] *Ibid.,* p. 185.
[57] *Ibid.,* p. 475.
[58] *Ibid.,* p. 185.
[59] "Whistler is right when he says in *Ten O'clock* that Art is distinct from
morality; and yet Ruskin, too, utters a truth, though on a different level, when
he says that all great art is a form of morality." Marcel Proust, *Correspondence
avec sa mère,* ed. Philip Kolb (Paris, 1953), p. 279. Quoted in George Painter,
Marcel Proust (London, 1965), II, 29–30.

My Memories of Oscar Wilde

by George Bernard Shaw

My Dear Harris:—

I have an interesting letter of yours to answer; but when you ask me to exchange biographies, you take an unfair advantage of the changes of scene and bustling movement of your own adventures. My autobiography would be like my best plays, fearfully long, and not divided into acts. Just consider this life of Wilde which you have just sent me, and which I finished ten minutes ago after putting aside everything else to read it at one stroke.

Why was Wilde so good a subject for a biography that none of the previous attempts which you have just wiped out are bad? Just because his stupendous laziness simplified his life almost as if he knew instinctively that there must be no episodes to spoil the great situation at the end of the last act but one. It was a well made life in the Scribe sense. It was as simple as the life of Des Grieux, Manon Lescaut's lover; and it beat that by omitting Manon and making Des Grieux his own lover and his own hero.

Des Grieux was a worthless rascal by all conventional standards; and we forgive him everything. We think we forgive him because he was unselfish and loved greatly. Oscar seems to have said: "I will love nobody: I will be utterly selfish; and I will be not merely a rascal but a monster; and you shall forgive me everything. In other words, I will reduce your standards to absurdity, not by writing them down, though I could do that so well—in fact, *have* done it —but by actually living them down and dying them down."

However, I musn't start writing a book to you about Wilde; I must just tumble a few things together and tell you them. To take things in the order of your book, I can remember only one occasion on which I saw Sir William Wilde, who, by the way, operated on my father to correct a squint, and overdid the corrections so much that my father squinted the other way all the rest of his life. To this day I never notice a squint; it is as normal to me as a nose or a tall hat.

I was a boy at a concert in the Ancient Concert Rooms in Brunswick Street in Dublin. Everybody was in evening dress; and—unless I am mixing up this concert with another (in which case I doubt if the Wildes would have been present)—the Lord Lieutenant was there with his blue waistcoated courtiers. Wilde was dressed in snuffy brown; and as he had the sort of skin that never looks clean, he produced a dramatic effect beside Lady Wilde (in full fig) of being, like Frederick the Great, Beyond Soap and Water, as his Nietzschean son was beyond Good and Evil. He was currently reported to have a family in every farmhouse; and the wonder was that Lady Wilde didn't mind—evidently a tradition from the Travers case, which I did not know about until I read your account, as I was only eight in 1864.

Lady Wilde was nice to me in London during the desperate days between my arrival in 1876 and my first earning of an income by my pen in 1885, or rather until, a few years earlier, I threw myself into Socialism and cut myself contemptuously loose from everything of which her at-homes—themselves desperate affairs enough, as you saw for yourself—were part. I was at two or three of them; and I once dined with her in company with an ex-tragedy queen named Miss Glynn, who, having no visible external ears, reared a head like a turnip. Lady Wilde talked about Schopenhauer; and Miss Glynn told me that Gladstone formed his oratorical style on Charles Kean.

I ask myself where and how I came across Lady Wilde; for we had no social relations in the Dublin days. The explanation must be that my sister, then a very attractive girl who sang beautifully, had met and made some sort of innocent conquest of both Oscar and Willie. I met Oscar once at one of the at-homes; and he came and spoke to me with an evident intention of being specially kind to me. We put each other out frightfully; and this odd difficulty persisted between us to the very last, even when we were no longer mere boyish novices and had become men of the world with plenty of skill in social intercourse. I saw him very seldom, as I avoided literary and artistic society like the plague, and refused the few invitations I received to go into society with burlesque ferocity, so as to keep out of it without offending people past their willingness to indulge me as a privileged lunatic.

The last time I saw him was at that tragic luncheon of yours at the Café Royal; and I am quite sure our total of meetings from first to last did not exceed twelve, and may not have exceeded six.

I definitely recollect six: (1) At the at-home aforesaid. (2) At Macmurdo's house in Fitzroy Street in the days of the Century Guild and its paper *The Hobby Horse*. (3) At a meeting somewhere in Westminster at which I delivered an address on Socialism, and at which Oscar turned up and spoke. Robert Ross surprised me greatly by telling me, long after Oscar's death, that it was this address of mine that moved Oscar to try his hand at a similar feat by writing "The Soul of Man Under Socialism." (4) A chance meeting near the stage door of the Haymarket Theatre, at which our queer shyness of one another made our resolutely cordial and appreciative conversation so difficult that our final laugh and shake-hands was almost a reciprocal confession. (5) A really pleasant afternoon we spent together on catching one another in a place where our presence was an absurdity. It was some exhibition in Chelsea; a naval commemoration, where there was a replica of Nelson's Victory and a set of P. & O. cabins which made one seasick by mere association of ideas. I don't know why I went or why Wilde went; but we did; and the question what the devil we were doing in that galley tickled us both. It was my sole experience of Oscar's wonderful gift as a raconteur. I remember particularly an amazingly elaborate story which you have no doubt heard from him; an example of the cumulation of a single effect, as in Mark Twain's story of the man who was persuaded to put lightning conductor after lightning conductor at every possible point on his roof until a thunderstorm came and all the lightning in the heavens went for his house and wiped it out.

Oscar's much more carefully and elegantly worked out story was of a young man who invented a theatre stall which economized space by ingenious contrivances which were all described. A friend of his invited twenty millionaires to meet him at dinner so that he might interest them in the invention. The young man convinced them completely by his demonstration of the saving in a theatre holding, in ordinary seats, six hundred people, leaving them eager and ready to make his fortune. Unfortunately he went on to calculate the annual saving in all the theatres of the world; then in all the churches of the world; then in all the legislatures; estimating finally the incidental and moral and religious effects of the invention until at the end of an hour he had estimated a profit of several thousand millions: the climax of course being that the millionaires folded their tents and silently stole away, leaving the ruined inventor a marked man for life.

Wilde and I got on extraordinarily well on this occasion. I had not to talk myself, but to listen to a man telling me stories better than I could have told them. We did not refer to Art, about which, excluding literature from the definition, he knew only what could be picked up by reading about it. He was in a tweed suit and low hat like myself, and had been detected and had detected me in the act of clandestinely spending a happy day at Rosherville Gardens instead of pontificating in his frock coat and so forth. And he had an audience on whom not one of his subtlest effects was lost. And so for once our meeting was a success; and I understood why Morris, when he was dying slowly, enjoyed a visit from Wilde more than from anybody else, as I understand why you say in your book that you would rather have Wilde back than any friend you have ever talked to, even though he was incapable of friendship, though not of the most touching kindness[1] on occasion.

Our sixth meeting, the only other one I can remember, was the one at the Café Royal. On that occasion he was not too preoccupied with his danger to be disgusted with me because I, who had praised his first plays handsomely, had turned traitor over "The Importance of Being Earnest." Clever as it was, it was his first really heartless play. In the others the chivalry of the eighteenth century Irishman and the romance of the disciple of Théophile Gautier (Oscar was really old-fashioned in the Irish way, except as a critic of morals) not only gave a certain kindness and gallantry to the serious passages and to the handling of the women, but provided that proximity of

[1] Excellent analysis. [F. H.]

emotion without which laughter, however irresistible, is destructive
and sinister. In "The Importance of Being Earnest" this had vanished; and the play, though extremely funny, was essentially hateful.
I had no idea that Oscar was going to the dogs, and that this represented a real degeneracy produced by his debaucheries. I thought
he was still developing; and I hazarded the unhappy guess that
"The Importance of Being Earnest" was in idea a young work written or projected long before under the influence of Gilbert and
furbished up for Alexander as a potboiler. At the Café Royal that
day I calmly asked him whether I was not right. He indignantly repudiated my guess, and said loftily (the only time he ever tried on
me the attitude he took to John Gray and his more abject disciples)
that he was disappointed in me. I suppose I said, "Then what on
earth has happened to you?" but I recollect nothing more on that
subject except that we did not quarrel over it.

When he was sentenced I spent a railway journey on a Socialist
lecturing excursion to the North drafting a petition for his release.
After that I met Willie Wilde at a theatre which I think must have
been the Duke of York's because I connect it vaguely with St. Martin's Lane. I spoke to him about the petition, asking him whether
anything of the sort was being done, and warning him that though
I and Stewart Headlam would sign it, that would be no use, as we
were two notorious cranks, and our names would by themselves reduce the petition to absurdity and do Oscar more harm than good.
Willie cordially agreed, and added, with maudlin pathos and an in-
conceivable want of tact: "Oscar was NOT a man of bad character:
you could have trusted him with a woman anywhere." He convinced
me, as you discovered later, that signatures would not be obtainable;
so the petition project dropped; and I don't know what became of
my draft.

When Wilde was in Paris during his last phase I made a point of
sending him inscribed copies of all my books as they came out; and
he did the same to me.

In writing about Wilde and Whistler, in the days when they were
treated as witty triflers, and called Oscar and Jimmy in print, I always made a point of taking them seriously and with scrupulous
good manners. Wilde on his part also made a point of recognizing
me as a man of distinction by his manner, and repudiating the cur-

rent estimate of me as a mere jester. This was not the usual recipro-
cal-admiration trick. I believe he was sincere, and felt indignant at
what he thought was a vulgar underestimate of me; and I had the
same feeling about him. My impulse to rally to him in his misfortune, and my disgust at "the man Wilde" scurrilities of the newspapers, was irresistible: I don't quite know why; for my charity to
his perversion, and my recognition of the fact that it does not imply
any general depravity or coarseness of character, came to me through
reading and observation, not through sympathy.

I have all the normal violent repugnance to homosexuality—if it
is really normal, which nowadays one is sometimes provoked to
doubt.

Also, I was in no way predisposed to like him. He was my fellow-
townsman, and a very prime specimen of the sort of fellow-towns-
man I most loathed: to wit, the Dublin snob. His Irish charm, po-
tent with Englishmen, did not exist for me; and on the whole it
may be claimed for him that he got no regard from me that he did
not earn.

What first established a friendly feeling in me was, unexpectedly
enough, the affair of the Chicago anarchists, whose Homer you con-
stituted yourself by *The Bomb*. I tried to get some literary men in
London, all heroic rebels and skeptics on paper, to sign a memorial
asking for the reprieve of these unfortunate men. The only signa-
ture I got was Oscar's. It was a completely disinterested act on his
part; and it secured my distinguished consideration for him for
the rest of his life.

To return for a moment to Lady Wilde. You know that there is
a disease called gigantism, caused by "a certain morbid process in
the sphenoid bone of the skull—viz., an excessive development of
the anterior lobe of the pituitary body" (this is from the nearest
encyclopedia). "When this condition does not become active until
after the age of twenty-five, by which time the long bones are con-
solidated, the result is acromegaly, which chiefly manifests itself in
an enlargement of the hands and feet." I never saw Lady Wilde's
feet; but her hands were enormous, and never went straight to their
aim when they grasped anything, but minced about, feeling for it.
And the gigantic splaying of her palm was reproduced in her lum-
bar region.

Now Oscar was an overgrown man, with something not quite normal about his bigness—something that made Lady Colin Campbell, who hated him, describe him as "that great white caterpillar." You yourself describe the disagreeable impression he made on you physically, in spite of his fine eyes and style. Well, I have always maintained that Oscar was a giant in the pathological sense, and that this explains a good deal of his weakness.

I think you have affectionately underrated his snobbery, mentioning only the pardonable and indeed justifiable side of it; the love of fine names and distinguished associations and luxury and good manners.[2] You say repeatedly, and *on certain planes*, truly, that he was not bitter and did not use his tongue to wound people. But this is not true on the snobbish plane. On one occasion he wrote about T. P. O'Connor with deliberate, studied, wounding insolence, with his Merrion Square Protestant pretentiousness in full cry against the Catholic. He repeatedly declaimed against the vulgarity of the British journalist, not as you or I might, but as an expression of the odious class feeling that is itself the vilest vulgarity. He made the mistake of not knowing his place. He objected to be addressed as Wilde, declaring that he was Oscar to his intimates and Mr. Wilde to others, quite unconscious of the fact that he was imposing on the men with whom, as a critic and journalist, he had to live and work, the alternative of granting him an intimacy he had no right to ask or a deference to which he had no claim. The vulgar hated him for snubbing them; and the valiant men damned his impudence and cut him. Thus he was left with a band of devoted satellites on the one hand, and a dining-out connection on the other, with here and there a man of talent and personality enough to command his respect, but utterly without that fortifying body of

---

[2] I had touched on the evil side of his snobbery, I thought, by saying that it was only famous actresses and great ladies that he ever talked about, and in telling how he loved to speak of the great houses such as Clumber to which he had been invited, and by half a dozen other hints scattered through my book. I had attacked English snobbery so strenuously in my book "The Man Shakespeare," had resented its influence on the finest English intelligence so bitterly, that I thought if I again laid stress on it in Wilde, people would think I was crazy on the subject. But he was a snob, both by nature and training, and I understand by snob what Shaw evidently understands by it here.

acquaintance among plain men in which a man must move as himself a plain man, and be Smith and Jones and Wilde and Shaw and Harris instead of Bosie and Robbie and Oscar and Mister. This is the sort of folly that does not last forever in a man of Wilde's ability; but it lasted long enough to prevent Oscar laying any solid social foundations.[3]

Another difficulty I have already hinted at. Wilde started as an apostle of Art; and in that capacity he was a humbug. The notion that a Portora boy, passed on to T.C.D. and thence to Oxford and spending his vacations in Dublin, could without special circumstances have any genuine intimacy with music and painting, is to me ridiculous.[4] When Wilde was at Portora, I was at home in a house where important musical works, including several typical masterpieces, were being rehearsed from the point of blank amateur ignorance up to fitness for public performance. I could whistle them from the first bar to the last as a butcher's boy whistles music hall songs, before I was twelve. The toleration of popular music— Strauss's waltzes, for instance—was to me positively a painful acquirement, a sort of republican duty.

I was so fascinated by painting that I haunted the National Gallery, which Doyle had made perhaps the finest collection of its size in the world; and I longed for money to buy painting materials with. This afterwards saved me from starving. It was as a critic of music and painting in the *World* that I won through my ten years of journalism before I finished up with you on the *Saturday Review*. I could make deaf stockbrokers read my two pages on music, the

---

[3] The reason that Oscar, snobbish as he was, and admirer of England and the English as he was, could not lay any solid social foundations in England was, in my opinion, his intellectual interests and his intellectual superiority to the men he met. No one with a fine mind devoted to things of the spirit is capable of laying solid social foundations in England. Shaw, too, has no solid social foundations in that country.

This passing shot at English society serves it right. Yet able men have found niches in London. Where was Oscar's?—G. B. S.

[4] I had already marked it down to put in my book that Wilde continually pretended to a knowledge of music which he had not got. He could hardly tell one tune from another, but he loved to talk of that "scarlet thing of Dvorak," hoping in this way to be accepted as a real critic of music, when he knew nothing about it and cared even less. His eulogies of music and painting betrayed him continually though he did not know it.

alleged joke being that I knew nothing about it. The real joke was that I knew all about it.

Now it was quite evident to me, as it was to Whistler and Beardsley, that Oscar knew no more about pictures[5] than anyone of his general culture and with his opportunities can pick up as he goes along. He could be witty about Art, as I could be witty about engineering; but that is no use when you have to seize and hold the attention and interest of people who really love music and painting. Therefore, Oscar was handicapped by a false start, and got a reputation[6] for shallowness and insincerity which he never retrieved until it was too late.

Comedy: the criticism of morals and manners *viva voce*, was his real forte. When he settled down to that he was great. But, as you found when you approached Meredith about him, his initial mistake had produced that "rather low opinion of Wilde's capacities," that "deep-rooted contempt for the showman in him," which persisted as a first impression and will persist until the last man who remembers his esthetic period has perished. The world has been in some ways so unjust to him that one must be careful not to be unjust to the world.

In the preface on education, called "Parents and Children," to my volume of plays beginning with *Misalliance*, there is a section headed "Artist Idolatry," which is really about Wilde. Dealing with "the powers enjoyed by brilliant persons who are also connoisseurs in art," I say, "the influence they can exercise on young people who have been brought up in the darkness and wretchedness of a home without art, and in whom a natural bent towards art has always been baffled and snubbed, is incredible to those who have not witnessed and understood it. He (or she) who reveals the world of art to them opens heaven to them. They become satellites, disciples, worshippers of the apostle. Now the apostle may be a voluptuary without much conscience. Nature may have given him enough virtue to suffice in a reasonable environment. But this allowance may not be enough to defend him against the temptation and demoral-

---

[5] I touched upon Oscar's ignorance of art sufficiently, I think, when I said in my book that he had learned all he knew of art and of controversy from Whistler, and that his lectures on the subject, even after sitting at the feet of the Master, were almost worthless.

[6] Perfectly true, and a notable instance of Shaw's insight.

ization of finding himself a little god on the strength of what ought to be a quite ordinary culture. He may find adorers in all directions in our uncultivated society among people of stronger character than himself, not one of whom, if they had been artistically educated, would have had anything to learn from him, or regarded him as in any way extraordinary apart from his actual achievements as an artist. Tartuffe is not always a priest. Indeed, he is not always a rascal; he is often a weak man absurdly credited with omniscience and perfection, and taking unfair advantages only because they are offered to him and he is too weak to refuse. Give everyone his culture, and no one will offer him more than his due."

That paragraph was the outcome of a walk and talk I had one afternoon at Chartres with Robert Ross.

You reveal Wilde as a weaker man than I thought him. I still believe that his fierce Irish pride had something to do with his refusal to run away from the trial. But in the main your evidence is conclusive. It was part of his tragedy that people asked more moral strength from him than he could bear the burden of, because they made the very common mistake—of which actors get the benefit—of regarding style as evidence of strength, just as in the case of women they are apt to regard paint as evidence of beauty. Now Wilde was so in love with style that he never realized the danger of biting off more than he could chew. In other words, of putting up more style than his matter would carry. Wise kings wear shabby clothes, and leave the gold lace to the drum major.

You do not, unless my memory is betraying me as usual, quite recollect the order of events just before the trial. That day at the Café Royal, Wilde said he had come to ask you to go into the witness box next day and testify that *Dorian Gray* was a highly moral work. Your answer was something like this: "For God's sake, man, put everything on that plane out of your head. You don't realize what is going to happen to you. It is not going to be a matter of clever talk about your books. They are going to bring up a string of witnesses that will put art and literature out of the question. Clarke will throw up his brief. He will carry the case to a certain point; and then, when he sees the avalanche coming, he will back out and leave you in the dock. What you have to do is to cross to France to-night. Leave a letter saying that you cannot face the squalor and horror of a law case; that you are an artist and unfitted for such things. Don't stay here clutching at straws like testimonials to *Dorian Gray*. *I tell you I know*. I know what is going to happen. I know Clarke's sort. I know what evidence they have got. You must go."

It was no use. Wilde was in a curious double temper. He made no pretence either of innocence or of questioning the folly of his proceedings against Queensberry. But he had an infatuate haughtiness as to the impossibility of his retreating, and as to his right to dictate your course. Douglas sat in silence, a haughly indignant silence, copying Wilde's attitude as all Wilde's admirers did, but quite probably influencing Wilde as you suggest, by the copy. Oscar finally rose with a mixture of impatience and his grand air, and walked out with the remark that he had now found out who were his real friends; and Douglas followed him, absurdly smaller, and imitating his walk, like a curate following an archbishop.[7] You remember it the other way about; but just consider this. Douglas was in the wretched position of having ruined Wilde merely to annoy his father, and of having attempted it so idiotically that he had actually prepared a triumph for him. He was, besides, much the youngest man present, and looked younger than he was. You did not make him welcome. As far as I recollect you did not greet him by a word or nod. If he had given the smallest provocation or attempted to take the lead in any way, I should not have given twopence for the chance of your keeping your temper. And Wilde, even in his ruin—which, however, he did not yet fully realize—kept his air of authority on questions of taste and conduct. It was practically impossible under such circumstances that Douglas should have taken the stage in any way. Everyone thought him a horrid little brat; but I, not having met him before to my knowledge, and having some sort of flair for his literary talent, was curious to hear what he had to say for himself. But, except to echo Wilde once or twice, he said noth-

[7] This is an inimitable picture, but Shaw's fine sense of comedy has misled him. The scene took place absolutely as I recorded it. Douglas went out first saying—"Your telling him to run away shows that you are no friend of Oscar's." Then Oscar got up to follow him. He said good-bye to Shaw, adding a courteous word or two. As he turned to the door I got up and said:—"I hope you do not doubt my friendship; you have no reason to."

"I do not think this is friendly of you, Frank," he said, and went on out.

ing.[8] You are right in effect, because it was evident that Wilde was in his hands, and was really echoing him. But Wilde automatically kept the prompter off the stage and himself in the middle of it.

What your book needs to complete it is a portrait of yourself as good as your portrait of Wilde. Oscar was not combative, though he was supercilious in his early pose. When his snobbery was not in action, he liked to make people devoted to him and to flatter them exquisitely with that end. Mrs. Calvert, whose great final period as a stage old woman began with her appearance in my *Arms and the Man*, told me one day, when apologizing for being, as she thought, a bad rehearser, that no author had ever been so nice to her except Mr. Wilde.

Pugnacious people, if they did not actually terrify Oscar, were at least the sort of people he could not control, and whom he feared as possibly able to coerce him. You suggest that the Queensberry pugnacity was something that Oscar could not deal with success- fully. But how in that case could Oscar have felt quite safe with you? You were more pugnacious than six Queensberrys rolled into one. When people asked, "What has Frank Harris been?" the usual reply was, "Obviously a pirate from the Spanish Main."

Oscar, from the moment he gained your attachment, could never have been afraid of what you might do to him, as he was sufficient of a connoisseur in Blut Bruderschaft to appreciate yours; but he must always have been mortally afraid of what you might do or say to his friends.[9]

You had quite an infernal scorn for nineteen out of twenty of the men and women you met in the circles he most wished to propitiate; and nothing could induce you to keep your knife in its sheath when they jarred on you. The Spanish Main itself would have blushed rosy red at your language when classical invective did not suffice to express your feelings.

[8] I am sure Douglas took the initiative and walked out first.

I have no doubt you are right, and that my vision of the exit is really a reminiscence of the entrance. In fact, now that you prompt my memory, I recall quite distinctly that Douglas, who came in as the follower, went out as the leader, and that the last word was spoken by Wilde after he had gone.—G. B. S.

[9] This insight on Shaw's part makes me smile because it is absolutely true. Oscar commended Bosie Douglas to me again and again and again, begged me to be nice to him if we ever met by chance; but I refused to meet him for months and months.

It may be that if, say, Edmund Gosse had come to Oscar when he was out on bail, with a couple of first class tickets in his pocket, and gently suggested a mild trip to Folkestone, or the Channel Islands, Oscar might have let himself be coaxed away. But to be called on to gallop *ventre à terre* to Erith—it might have been Deal —and hoist the Jolly Roger on board your lugger, was like casting a light comedian and first lover for *Richard III*. Oscar could not see himself in the part.

I must not press the point too far; but it illustrates, I think, what does not come out at all in your book: that you were a very different person from the submissive and sympathetic disciples to whom he was accustomed. There are things more terrifying to a soul like Oscar's than an as yet unrealized possibility of a sentence of hard labour. A voyage with Captain Kidd may have been one of them. Wilde was a conventional man; his unconventionality was the very pedantry of convention; never was there a man less an outlaw than he. You were a born outlaw, and will never be anything else.

That is why, in his relations with you, he appears as a man always shirking action—more of a coward (all men are cowards more or less) than so proud a man can have been. Still this does not affect the truth and power of your portrait. Wilde's memory will have to stand or fall by it.

You will be blamed, I imagine, because you have not written a lying epitaph instead of a faithful chronicle and study of him; but you will not lose your sleep over that. As a matter of fact, you could not have carried kindness further without sentimental folly. I should have made a far sterner summing up. I am sure Oscar has not found the gates of heaven shut against him. He is too good company to be excluded; but he can hardly have been greeted as, "Thou good and faithful servant." The first thing we ask a servant for is a testimonial to honesty, sobriety and industry; for we soon find out that these are the scarce things, and that geniuses[10] and clever people are as common as rats. Well, Oscar was not sober, not

[10] The English paste in Shaw; genius is about the rarest thing on earth whereas the necessary quantum of "honesty, sobriety and industry," is beaten by life into nine humans out of ten—F. H.

If so, it is the tenth who comes my way.—G. B. S.

honest, not industrious. Society praised him for being idle, and persecuted him savagely for an aberration which it had better have left unadvertized, thereby making a hero of him; for it is in the nature of people to worship those who have been made to suffer horribly. Indeed I have often said that if the crucifixion could be proved a myth, and Jesus convicted of dying of old age in comfortable circumstances, Christianity would lose ninety-nine per cent of its devotees.

We must try to imagine what judgment we should have passed on Oscar if he had been a normal man, and had dug his grave with his teeth in the ordinary respectable fashion, as his brother Willie did. This brother, by the way, gives us some cue; for Willie, who had exactly the same education and the same chances, must be ruthlessly set aside by literary history as a vulgar journalist of no account. Well, suppose Oscar and Willie had both died the day before Queensberry left that card at the Club! Oscar would still have been remembered as a wit and a dandy, and would have had a niche beside Congreve in the drama. A volume of his aphorisms would have stood creditably on the library shelf with La Rochefoucauld's Maxims. We should have missed the "Ballad of Reading Gaol" and "De Profundis"; but he would still have cut a considerable figure in the Dictionary of National Biography, and been read and quoted outside the British Museum reading room.

As to the "Ballad" and "De Profundis," I think it is greatly to Oscar's credit that, whilst he was sincere and deeply moved when he was protesting against the cruelty of our present system to children and to prisoners generally, he could not write about his own individual share in that suffering with any conviction or sympathy.[11] Except for the passage where he describes his exposure at Clapham Junction, there is hardly a line in "De Profundis" that he might not have written as a literary feat five years earlier. But in the "Ballad," even in borrowing form and melody from Coleridge, he shews that he could pity others when he could not seriously pity himself. And this, I think, may be pleaded against the reproach that he was selfish. Externally, in the ordinary action of life as distinguished from the literary action proper to his genius, he was no doubt sluggish and weak because of his gigantism. He ended

[11] Superb criticism.

as an unproductive drunkard and swindler; for the repeated sales of the Daventry plot, in so far as they imposed on the buyers and were not transparent excuses for begging, were undeniably swindles. For all that, he does not appear in his writings a selfish or base-minded man. He is at his worst and weakest in the suppressed [12] part of "De Profundis"; but in my opinion it had better be published, for several reasons. It explains some of his personal weakness by the stifling narrowness of his daily round, ruinous to a man whose proper place was in a large public life. And its concealment is mischievous because, first, it leads people to imagine all sorts of horrors in a document which contains nothing worse than any record of the squabbles of two touchy idlers; and, second, it is clearly a monstrous thing that Douglas should have a torpedo launched at him and timed to explode after his death. The torpedo is a very harmless squib; for there is nothing in it that cannot be guessed from Douglas's own book; but the public does not know that. By the way, it is rather a humorous stroke of Fate's irony that the son of the Marquis of Queensberry should be forced to expiate his sins by suffering a succession of blows beneath the belt.

Now that you have written the best life of Oscar Wilde, let us have the best life of Frank Harris. Otherwise the man behind your works will go down to posterity[13] as the hero of my very inadequate preface to "The Dark Lady of the Sonnets."

G. BERNARD SHAW.

[12] I have said this in my way.

[13] A characteristic flirt of Shaw's humour. He is a great caricaturist and not a portrait-painter.

When he thinks of my Celtic face and aggressive American frankness he talks of me as pugnacious and a pirate: "a Captain Kidd." In his preface to "The Fair Lady of the Sonnets" he praises my "idiosyncratic gift of pity"; says that I am "wise through pity"; then he extols me as a prophet, not seeing that a pitying sage, prophet and pirate constitute an inhuman superman.

I shall do more for Shaw than he has been able to do for me; he is the first figure in my new volume of "Contemporary Portraits." I have portrayed him there at his best, as I love to think of him, and henceforth he'll have to try to live up to my conception and that will keep him, I'm afraid, on strain.

God help me!—G. B. S.

The Unimportance of Being Oscar

by Mary McCarthy

One of Oscar Wilde's acquaintances wrote of him that he could never be quite a gentleman because he dressed too well and his manners were too polished. The same criticism can be made of his art. There is something *outré* in all of Wilde's work that makes one sympathize to a degree with the Marquess of Queensberry; this fellow is really insufferable. Oscar's real sin (and the one for which society punished him, homosexuality being merely the blotter charge) was making himself too much at home. This is as readily seen in his comedies as in his epigrammatic indorsement of socialism or his call on a Colorado coal mine. He was overly familiar with his subjects. Shaw said of him that he did not know enough about art to justify his parade of aestheticism. Certainly, he was not intimate enough with poverty to style himself an enemy of riches. In this light, the Marquess of Queensberry's libel, that he went about "posing" as a sodomist, speaks, in the plain man's language, the true word of damnation. In his comedies, it is his audience whose acquaintance he presumes on. Where the usual work of art invites the spectator into its world, already furnished and habitable, Wilde's plays do just the opposite: the author invites himself and his fast opinions into the world of the spectator. He ensconces himself with intolerable freedom and always outstays his sufferance— the trouble with Wilde's wit is that it does not recognize when the party is over. The effect of this effrontery is provoking in both

"The Unimportance of Being Oscar." From *Mary McCarthy's Theatre Chronicles* by Mary McCarthy (New York: Farrar, Straus & Company, 1963), pp. 106–10, the major portion of which book was originally published in 1956 as *Sights and Spectacles*. Reprinted with permission of Farrar, Straus & Giroux, Inc. from *Sights and Spectacles* by Mary McCarthy. Copyright © 1947, 1956, 1963 by Mary McCarthy.

senses; the outrageous has its own monotony, and insolence can only strike once.

In *The Importance of Being Earnest* (Royale Theatre), the tedium is concentrated in the second act, where two young ladies are rude to each other over tea and cake, and two young gentlemen follow them being selfish about the muffins. The joke of gluttony and the joke of rudeness (which are really the same one, for heartlessness is the basic pleasantry) have been exhausted in the first act: nothing can be said by the muffin that has not already been said by the cucumber sandwich. The thin little joke that remains, the importance of the name Ernest for matrimony, is in its visible aspects insufficiently entertaining. That the joke about the name Ernest is doubtless a private one makes it less endurable to the audience, which is pointedly left out of the fun. To the bisexual man, it was perhaps deliciously comic that a man should have one name, the tamest in English, for his wife and female relations, and another for his male friends, for trips and "lost" weekends; but Wilde was a prude—he went to law to clear his character—and the antisocial jibe dwindles on the stage to a refined and incomprehensible titter.

Yet, in spite of the exhausting triviality of the second act, *The Importance of Being Earnest* is Wilde's most original play. It has the character of a ferocious idyl. Here, for the first time, the subject of Wilde's comedy coincides with its climate; there is no more pretense of emotion. The unwed mother, his stock "serious" heroine, here becomes a stock joke—"Shall there be a different standard for women than for men?" cries Mr. Jack Worthing, flinging himself on the governess, Miss Prism, who had checked him accidentally in a valise at a railroad station twenty-five years before. In *The Importance of Being Earnest* the title is a *blague,* and virtue disappears from the Wilde stage, as though jerked off by one of those hooks that were used in the old days of vaudeville to remove an unsuccessful performer. Depravity is the hero and the only character, the people on the stage embodying various shades of it. It is deepest dyed in the pastoral region of respectability and innocence. The London *roué* is artless simplicity itself beside the dreadnought society dowager, and she, in her turn, is out-brazened by her debutante daughter, and she by the country miss, and she by her spectacled governess, till finally the village rector with his clerical clothes, his vow of celibacy, and his sermon on the manna, adjustable to all occasions, slithers noiselessly into the rose garden, specious as the Serpent Himself.

The formula of this humor is the same as that of the detective story: the culprit is the man with the most guileless appearance. Normal expectations are methodically inverted, and the structure of the play is the simple structure of the paradox. Like the detective story, like the paradox, this play is a shocker. It is pure sport of the mind, and hence very nearly "English." The clergyman is the fox; the governess the vixen; and the young bloods are out for the kill. Humanitarian considerations are out of place here; they belong to the middle class. Insensibility is the comic "vice" of the characters; it is also their charm and badge of prestige. Selfishness and servility are the moral alternatives presented; the sinister impression made by the governess and the rector comes partly from their rectitude and partly from their menial demeanor. Algernon Moncrieff and Cecily Cardew are, taken by themselves, unendurable; the meeching Dr. Chasuble, however, justifies their way of life by affording a comparison—it is better to be cruel than craven.

Written on the brink of his fall, *The Importance of Being Earnest* is Wilde's true *De Profundis*; the other was false sentiment. This is hell, and if a great deal of it is tiresome, eternity is, as M. Sartre says, a bore. The tone of the Wilde dialogue, inappropriate to the problem drama, perfectly reflects conditions in this infernal Arcadia; peevish, fretful, valetudinarian, it is the tone of an elderly recluse who lives imprisoned by his comforts; it combines the finicky and the greedy, like a piggish old lady.

Fortunately, however, for everyone, there is a goddess in the play. The great lumbering dowager, Lady Augusta Bracknell, traveling to the country in a luggage-train, is the only character thick and rudimentary enough to be genuinely well-born. Possibly because of her birth, she has a certain Olympian freedom. When she is on the stage—during the first and the third acts—the play opens up. The epigram, which might be defined as the *desire* to say something witty, falters before her majesty. Her own rumbling speech is unpredictable; anything may come out of her. Where the other

Mary McCarthy

characters are hard as nails, Lady Augusta is rock. She is so in-
sensitive that the spoken word reaches her slowly, from an im-
measurable distance, as if she were deaf. Into this splendid creation,
Wilde surely put all the feelings of admiration and despair aroused
in him by Respectability. This citadel of the arbitrary was for him
the Castle; he remarked, in his later years, that he would have been
glad to marry Queen Victoria. Lady Augusta is the one character
he could ever really imagine, partly, no doubt, because she could
not imagine *him*. Her effrontery surpasses his by being perfectly
unconscious; she cannot impose on the audience for she does not
know they are there. She is named, oddly enough, after Bracknell,
the country address of the Marchioness of Queensberry, where
Wilde, as it turned out, was less at home than he fancied. The irony
of the pastoral setting was apparently not lost on the Marquess of
Queensberry, who arrived at the first night with a bunch of turnips
and carrots.

The Importance of Being Earnest

by Eric Bentley

The Importance of Being Earnest (1895) is a variant, not of domestic drama like *Candida* or of melodrama like *Brassbound,* but of farce, a genre which, being the antithesis of serious, is not easily put to serious uses. In fact nothing is easier than to handle this play without noticing what it contains. It is so consistently farcical in tone, characterization, and plot that very few care to root out any more serious content. The general conclusion has been that Wilde merely decorates a silly play with a flippant wit. Like Shaw he is dismissed as "not really a dramatist at all." Unlike Shaw he does not have any such dramatic structure to offer in refutation of his critics as underlies a *Major Barbara* or a *Candida.* We cannot turn to him for the dialectical steel frame of a Molière or a Shaw. Yet we shall only display our own insensitivity if we dismiss him.

Insensitivity to slight and delicate things is insensitivity *tout court.* That is what Wilde meant when he declared that the man who despises superficiality is himself superficial. His best play is connected with this idea. As its title confesses, it is about *earnestness,* that is, Victorian solemnity, that kind of false seriousness which means priggishness, hypocrisy, and lack of irony. Wilde proclaims that earnestness is less praiseworthy than the ironic attitude to life which is regarded as superficial. His own art, and the comic spirit which Congreve embodied and which Meredith had described, were thereby vindicated. Wilde calls *The Importance of Being Earnest* "a trivial comedy for serious people" meaning, in the first place, a comedy which will be thought negligible by the earnest and, in the second, a *comedy of surface* for connoisseurs. The latter will perceive

"*The Importance of Being Earnest.*" From *The Playwright as Thinker* by Eric Bentley (New York: Reznal & Hitchcock, 1946), pp. 172–77. Copyright 1946 by Eric Bentley. Reprinted by permission of Harcourt, Brace & World, Inc.

that Wilde is as much of a moralist as Bernard Shaw but that, instead of presenting the problems of modern society directly, he flits around them, teasing them, declining to grapple with them. His wit is no searchlight into the darkness of modern life. It is a flickering, a coruscation, intermittently revealing the upper class of England in a harsh bizarre light. This upper class could feel about Shaw that at least he took them seriously, no one more so. But the outrageous Oscar (whom they took care to get rid of as they had got rid of Byron) refused to see the importance of being earnest.

One does not find Wilde's satire embedded in plot and character as in traditional high comedy. It is a running accompaniment to the play, and this fact, far from indicating immaturity, is the making of a new sort of comedy. The plot is one of those Gilbertian absurdities of lost infants and recovered brothers which can only be thought of to be laughed at. Yet the dialogue which sustains the plot, or is sustained by it, is an unbroken stream of comment on all the themes of life which the plot is so far from broaching. Perhaps *comment* is too flat and downright a conception. Wildean "comment" is a pseudo-irresponsible jabbing at all the great problems, and we would be justified in removing the prefix "pseudo" if the Wildean satire, for all its naughtiness, had not a cumulative effect and a paradoxical one. Flippancies repeated, developed, and, so to say, elaborated almost into a system amount to something in the end—and thereby cease to be flippant. What begins as a prank ends as a criticism of life. What begins as intellectual high-kicking ends as intellectual sharp-shooting.

The margins of an annotated copy of *The Importance* would show such headings as: death; money and marriage; the nature of style; ideology and economics; beauty and truth; the psychology of philanthropy; the decline of aristocracy; nineteenth-century morals; the class system. The possibility of such notations in itself means little. But if we bear in mind that Wilde is skimming steadily over mere topics all through *The Importance,* we can usefully turn to a particular page to see precisely how this works. To choose the opening page is not to load the dice in a dramatist's favor, since that page is usually either heavy-going exposition or mere patter which allows the audience to get seated. Here is Wilde's first page:

Algernon. Did you hear what I was playing, Lane?

Lane. I didn't think it polite to listen, sir.

Algernon. I'm sorry for that, for your sake. I don't play accurately—anyone can play accurately—but I play with wonderful expression. As far as the piano is concerned sentiment is my forte. I keep science for life.

Lane. Yes, sir.

Algernon. And, speaking of the science of Life, have you got the cucumber sandwiches cut for Lady Bracknell?

Lane. Yes, sir.

Algernon. Oh! . . . by the way, Lane, I see from your book that on Thursday night, when Lord Sherman and Mr. Worthing were dining with me, eight bottles of champagne are entered as having been consumed.

Lane. Yes, sir; eight bottles and a pint.

Algernon. Why is it that at a bachelor's establishment the servants invariably drink the champagne? I ask merely for information.

Lane. I attribute it to the superior quality of the wine, sir. I have often observed that in married households the champagne is rarely of a first-rate brand.

Algernon. Good heavens! Is marriage so demoralizing as that?

Lane. I believe it *is* a very pleasant state, sir. I have had very little experience of it myself up to the present. I have only been married once. That was in consequence a misunderstanding between myself and a young person.

Algernon. I don't know that I am much interested in your family life, Lane.

Lane. No, sir. It is not a very interesting subject. I never think of it myself.

Algernon. Very natural, I am sure. That will do, Lane, thank you.

Lane. Thank you, sir. (*He goes out*)

Algernon. Lane's views on marriage seem somewhat lax. Really, if the lower orders don't set us a good example, what on earth is the use of them? They seem, as a class, to have absolutely no sense of moral responsibility.

This passage is enough to show the way in which Wilde attaches a serious and satirical allusion to every remark. The butler's "I didn't think it polite to listen, sir" is a prelude to the jokes against class society which run through the play. Algernon's first little speech touches on the foolish opposition of life and sentiment, science and art. Talk of science and life leads by Wildean transition back to the action and the cucumber sandwiches. Champagne takes the action to speculation on servants and masters, and thence to marriage and morals. A little dialectical climax is reached with the answer to the question: "Is marriage so demoralizing as that?" when Lane coolly replies: "I believe it *is* a very pleasant state, sir," and adds, by way of an explanation no less disconcerting by Victorian standards, "I have had very little experience of it myself up to the present. I have only been married once." Which is followed by the explanation of the explanation: "That was in consequence of a misunderstanding. . . ." It cannot be said that marriage in this passage receives the "staggering blows" which the ardent reformer is wont to administer. But does it not receive poisoned pin pricks that are just as effective? Are not the inversions and double inversions of standards managed with dexterous delicacy? "No, sir. It is not a very interesting subject." A delicious turn in the argument! And then the little moralistic summing-up of Algernon's: "Lane's views on marriage seem somewhat lax. Really, if the lower orders don't set us a good example . . ." And so it ripples on.

We are accustomed to plays in which a serious plot and theme are enlivened—"dramatized," as we say—by comic incident and witticism. Such plays are at best sweetened pills. "Entertainment value" is added as an afterthought, reminding one of the man who, having watched for weeks the construction of a modern Gothic building, cried one day: "Oh, look, they're putting the architecture on now!" Oscar Wilde's procedure is the opposite of all this. He has no serious plot, no credible characters. His witticisms are, not comic, but serious relief. They are in ironic counterpoint with the absurdities of the action. This counterpoint is Wilde's method. It is what gives him his peculiar voice and his peculiar triumph. It is what makes him hard to catch: the fish's tail flicks, flashes, and disappears. Perhaps *The Importance* should be defined as "almost a satire." As the conversations in *Alice in Wonderland* hover on the frontier of sense without ever quite crossing it, so the dialogue in *The Importance* is forever on the frontier of satire, forever on the point of breaking into bitter criticism. In never breaks. The ridiculous action constantly steps in to prevent the break. That is its function. Before the enemy can denounce Wilde the agile outburst is over and we are back among the cucumber sandwiches.

The counterpoint or irony of Wilde's play expresses itself theatrically in the contrast between the elegance and *savoir-faire* of the actors and the absurdity of what they actually do. This contrast too can be dismissed as mere Oscarism and frivolity. Actually it is integral to an uncommonly rich play. The contrast between smooth, assured appearances and inner emptiness is, moreover, nothing more nor less than a fact of sociology and history. Wilde knew his England. He knew her so well that he could scarcely be surprised when she laughed off his truisms as paradoxes and fastened a humorless and baleful eye on all his flights of fancy. Wilde had his own solution to the problem stated by Meredith, the problem of finding a vantage point for satire in an unaristocratic age. It was the solution of Bohemianism. For Wilde the Bohemian attitude was far from being a philosophy in itself—a point which most of his friends and enemies, beginning at the Wilde trial, seem to have missed. Bohemianism was for Wilde a mask. To wear masks was Wilde's personal adjustment to modern life, as it was Nietzsche's. Hence we are right in talking of his pose as we are right in talking of Nietzsche's vanity. The mistake is in believing that these men deceived themselves. If we patronize them the joke is on us. If Wilde seems shallow when we want depth, if he seems a liar when we want truth, we should recall his words: "A Truth in Art is that whose contradictory is also true. The Truths of metaphysics are the Truths of masks." These words lead us to Pirandello.

An Improbable Life

by W. H. Auden

When we were young, most of us were taught that it is dishonorable to read other people's letters without their consent, and I do not think we should ever, even if we grow up to be literary scholars, forget this early lesson. The mere fact that a man is famous and dead does not entitle us to read, still less to publish, his private correspondence. We have to ask ourselves two questions —firstly, "Would he mind?," and, secondly, "Are the contents of such historical importance as to justify publication even if he would?" In the case of the born letter writer, like Horace Walpole, to whom letter writing is as natural and "impersonal" a form of literary composition as poetry or fiction, one generally feels that he would be pleased to have his letters read by the public, and in the case of men of action—statesmen, generals, and the like, whose decisions have affected the history of the society in which they lived —we are entitled to know anything about their lives that sheds light upon their public acts. Writers and artists, however, are another matter. Some of them have been born letter writers as well, but the average productive poet or novelist or dramatist is too busy, too self-centered, to spend much time and trouble over his correspondence; if and when he does, the letters are probably love letters and, since knowledge of an artist's private life never throws any significant light upon his work, there is no justification for intruding upon his privacy. Keats' letters to Fanny Brawne, and Beethoven's to his nephew, should either not have been published at all or, like psychological case histories, have been published anonymously.

What, then, about the letters of Oscar Wilde? Is their publication

"An Improbable Life" (review of *Letters of Oscar Wilde*) by W. H. Auden. From *The New Yorker,* 39:3 (March 9, 1963). Copyright 1963 by The New Yorker Magazine, Inc. Reprinted by permission of Curtis Brown, Ltd.

justified? Somewhat to my surprise, I find myself saying yes. Yeats said of Wilde that he seemed to be a man of action rather than a writer. What Yeats should have said, I think, is that Wilde was, both by genius and by fate, primarily an "actor," a performer. Even those of his contemporaries who most admired his writings admitted that they were inferior to his conversation; what inspired his imagination most was a physically present audience and its immediate response. From the beginning Wilde performed his life and continued to do so even after fate had taken the plot out of his hands. Drama is essentially revelation; on the stage no secrets are kept. I feel therefore, that there is nothing Wilde would desire more than that we should know everything about him. There remains the question of the recipients of his letters. They could not have been published until many of his most intimate friends—Alfred Douglas, Robbie Ross, Reggie Turner, More Adey, and others—were dead, because of the allusions to their homosexuality that they contain. With one exception, the revelation of what was in any case an open secret would not embarrass them in the least, and it is a trivial matter compared with what these letters reveal of their loyalty, compassion, and generosity toward Wilde at a time when to be his friend required great moral courage. The exception is, of course, Lord Alfred Douglas, who emerges from these letters as a vicious, gold-digging, snobbish, anti-Semitic, untalented little horror for whom no good word can be said. One might feel sorry for him if, after the catastrophe, he had kept his mouth shut, but he did not. He not only wrote an account of their relationship that is full of lies but also dared to put on virtuous airs, and it is only just that he should be exposed for what he was.

As all the reviewers have rightly pointed out, Mr. Rupert Hart-Davis, who has put together "The Letters of Oscar Wilde," now published by Harcourt, Brace & World, has done a masterly editorial job and one that must have been fiendishly difficult. Wilde's handwriting became very hard to read, he seldom dated his letters, few of his early biographers are to be trusted on matters of fact, some of the letters have been mutilated, and a number of forged ones exist. Out of the twelve hundred and ninety-eight letters Mr. Hart-Davis succeeded in collecting, he has printed all but two hundred unimportant brief notes. His own footnotes and index provide all the background information one could desire, and I have never read a work of this kind in which it was so easy to refind a note or make a cross-reference.

Wilde's life was a drama, and in reading his letters chronologically there is an excitement similar to that of watching a Greek tragedy in which the audience knows what is going to happen while the hero does not. The play begins, idyllically, in Oxford during the eighteen-seventies. Onstage are Wilde and two nice-looking fellow-undergraduates, Reginald Harding and William Ward, one destined to become a stockbroker, the other a solicitor in Bristol. Remembering my own years at Oxford, I would have expected Wilde's letters to them to be full of references to literary discoveries, of extravagant praise of this author and violent denunciations of that, or of philosophical arguments. But they are neither literary nor intellectual. There is scarcely a word in them about the "modern" poets of the time, like Swinburne, Morris, Rossetti, James Thomson, Coventry Patmore. Indeed, the only poem he speaks of with enthusiasm is, of all things, Mrs. Browning's "Aurora Leigh," which he ranks with "Hamlet" and "In Memoriam," and if his comment on the poem were to be quoted anonymously, I do not think anybody would guess the author:

> It is one of those books that, written straight from the heart—and such a large heart too—never weary one: because they are sincere. We tire of art but not of nature after all our aesthetic training.

This lack of interest in what others are writing and, on the rare occasion when interest is taken, the lack of perceptive critical judgment are characteristic of Wilde's letters up to the end. Of the poets who were beginning to publish between 1880 and 1899, only four —Bridges, Kipling, Yeats, and Housman—have really survived. (Myself, I would add Canon Dixon and Alice Meynell, but they are not widely read nor likely to be.) Wilde never mentions Bridges' nor Kipling's poetry, Yeats he knew personally and presumably read, Housman sent him a copy of "A Shropshire Lad," the manner and matter of which one would have expected to be exceptionally congenial to him, but he never seems to have realized that their poetry was in a completely different class from that of, say, Dowson or Le Gallienne. Nor was it, I think, personal infatuation that made him so absurdly overestimate Douglas's versified drivel; he quite honestly thought it was good. As a critic of drama he was a little better. He recognized the genius of Ibsen and—even more surprisingly, considering the difference in their views of art—that of Shaw. At a time when he was the most successful playwright in England and "Widowers' Houses" had just been hooted off the stage, Wilde had the insight and generosity to rank it with his own plays and say:

> I have read it twice with the keenest interest. I like your superb confidence in the dramatic value of the mere facts of life. I admire the horrible flesh and blood of your creatures, and your preface is a masterpiece—a real masterpiece of trenchant writing and caustic wit and dramatic instinct.

To return to his early letters. Their contents are for the most part affectionate personal chat, and almost the only impersonal topic is the aesthetic beauty of Roman Catholicism; flirtation with Rome seems to have been fashionable in Oxford at the time:

> If I *could hope* that the Church would wake in me some earnestness and purity I would go over *as a luxury,* if for no better reason. But I can hardly hope it would, and to go over to Rome would be to sacrifice and give up my two great gods "Money and Ambition."

The Oxford scene closes with Wilde's attainment of his immediate ambition, a First in Mods and Greats—a feat nobody, however brilliant, can bring off without much hard work. Now he goes up to London, takes rooms with a painter, Frank Miles, and within three years has become a friend of famous beauties like Lily Langtry, published a volume of poems (he sent a complimentary copy to Gladstone), and made himself one of the most talked-of persons in town. In April of 1881, Gilbert and Sullivan's "Patience" had its première; according to Mr. Hart-Davis, Gilbert may originally have had Rossetti in mind as the model for Bunthorne, but the public certainly took him to be a caricature of Wilde.

Except for those written from America, one cannot say that, taken as a whole, the letters Wilde wrote up till the time of his imprisonment are particularly interesting in their subject matter, or, knowing his extraordinary conversational powers, particularly funny. Wilde, that is to say, was a born talker, not a born letter writer—a

master of the improvised word in response to the spur of the moment. Compared with speech, even the most casual letter is con-
trived, and its writer cannot be present to witness the response of
the audience for whom he is writing. During the years of his social
and literary triumphs, Wilde always had an audience for his conversation, and therefore most of his letters were written not for
the sake of writing one but because a letter was called for; some-
body else's letter had to be answered, an editor had to be consulted,
a contribution to a magazine had to be solicited, etc. Nevertheless,
they make a very agreeable impression: they convince one that the
writer was a gracious, affectionate, generous, and, above all, kind-
hearted man, without the least malice or literary envy, and when
one considers how malicious most witty people are and how un-
generous and envious most writers are, one is filled with admiration.

In 1881, "Patience" opened in New York, and D'Oyly Carte's
American manager, Colonel Morse, thinking that Wilde's presence
would provide useful publicity, booked him for a lecture tour
through the United States. How big a name he already was at the
age of twenty-eight may be gauged from the fees he could command: in Boston and Chicago he got a thousand dollars for a
lecture, and he never got less than two hundred. (When I think
what the dollar was worth then, it makes *me* green with envy.) Almost immediately he became involved in a highly publicized and
comic quarrel with a rival British lecturer, Archibald Forbes. Wilde,
wearing knee breeches, a tight velvet doublet, and hair almost down
to his shoulders, was lecturing on Decorative Art in America and
the English Renaissance; Forbes, with closely cropped hair and his
chest covered with military medals, was lecturing on his adventures
as a war correspondent in the Balkans. It seems that the more
manly prima donna was the lesser draw; at any rate, it was Forbes
who picked the quarrel—Wilde did everything he could to placate
him—and the press had a field day. Many of the papers were hostile
to Wilde, but he could always win over an audience, even so unlikely a one as the miners of Leadville, Colorado, to whom he talked
about Benvenuto Cellini. Afterward there was a banquet under-
ground:

The amazement of the miners when they saw that art and appetite could go hand in hand knew no bounds; when I lit a long cigar they cheered till the silver fell in dust from the roof on our plates; and when I quaffed a cocktail without flinching, they unanimously pronounced me in their grand simple way "a bully boy with no glass eye." . . . Then I had to open a new vein, or lode, which with a silver drill I brilliantly performed, amidst unanimous applause. The silver drill was presented to me and the lode named "The Oscar."

It is interesting for the reader today to learn that Wilde stayed with Jefferson Davis in the South, and that he was in St. Joseph, Missouri, the week after Jesse James was shot; the reader also feels his first shivers of pity and fear. In Lincoln, Nebraska, his hosts

drove me out to see the great prison afterwards! Poor odd types of humanity in hideous striped dresses making bricks in the sun, and all mean-looking, which consoled me, for I should hate to see a criminal with a noble face.

and in Chicago he talks to the journalists about three of his heroes —Whistler, Labouchère, and Irving. The second of these was responsible for the amendment to the criminal laws under which Wilde was to be convicted, and after the sentence he publicly expressed his regret that the maximum sentence had not been made seven years instead of only two.

On his return, in 1883, Wilde spent three months in Paris, where he met one of his future biographers, Robert Sherard. In November he became engaged to Constance Lloyd and in the following May he married her. This was certainly the most immoral and perhaps the only really heartless act of Wilde's life. It can happen that a homosexual does not recognize his condition for a number of years and marries in good faith, but one cannot believe that Wilde was such an innocent. Most homosexuals enjoy the company of women and, since they are not tempted to treat them as sexual objects, can be most sympathetic and understanding friends to them; like normal men, many of them long for the comfort and security of a home and the joy of having children, but to marry for such reasons is heartless. I have never seen a marriage of this kind—at least if the partners were under fifty—in which the wife, even when she knew

all about her husband's tastes, did not suffer acutely. Even if there
had been no scandal to bring public humiliation upon her and
disgrace on their children, Constance Wilde would have been very
unhappy, because she must have felt that her husband was, as he
himself admitted later, "bored to death with married life." With a
wife and, presently, two children to support, Wilde was now faced
with the problem of securing a steady income. His first idea, oddly,
was to become, like Matthew Arnold, a school inspector. When this
failed to materialize, he took on the editorship of *Woman's World*.
His letters from this period show him to have been a conscientious
and hard-working editor. He even wrote to Queen Victoria to ask
if she had any poems written in her youth that he might have the
honor of publishing, and her minute concerning this request still
exists:

> Really what will people not say and invent. Never did the Queen in
> her whole life write *one line* of *poetry* serious or comic or make a
> *Rhyme* even. This is therefore all *invention* & a *myth*.

As a writer he turned, fortunately for all concerned, from poetry
to prose, and by 1889 was doing sufficiently well to give up being an
editor and live by his pen. "The Picture of Dorian Gray" caused
a scandal but sold well. "Salomé" was banned, but the four plays
he wrote between 1891 and 1894 were all of them stage triumphs
and made him the most admired and richest dramatist of his day.
During these years of mounting success, the names of the principal
characters in his drama make their entrance—Ross, Leonard Smithers, Turner, Adey, Frank Harris, Ada Leverson (whose novels,
incidentally, are now shamefully neglected), and, of course, Bosie
Douglas. The first warning note of doom is heard in 1894, when
Alfred Taylor, who ran a male whorehouse that Wilde frequented,
is arrested. This time the charge is dismissed, but less than a year
later they will be standing in the dock together. Whatever his vices,
Taylor will be remembered forever as a man of honor, for he went
to prison rather than turn Queen's Evidence.

Thanks to the movies, everyone is familiar with the details of
the three trials. Whether a law which makes homosexual acts between consenting adults a crime be just or unjust is debatable.

What is unarguable fact is, firstly, that such a law encourages the crime of blackmail and, secondly, that it is unenforceable; that is to say, to ninety-nine per cent of practicing homosexuals, it makes no difference, so far as their personal liberty is concerned, whether such a law be on the statute book or not. Of the one per cent or less who get into trouble, nearly all are either persons with a taste for very young boys, one of whom sooner or later tells his parents, or compulsive cruisers of public conveniences who sooner or later run into an *agent provocateur*. But for his incredible folly in suing Queensberry, Wilde would have been perfectly safe. As he himself wrote later to Douglas:

> Do you think I am here on account of my relations with the witnesses on my trial? My relations, real or supposed, with people of that kind were matters of no interest to either the Government or Society. They knew nothing of them, and cared less. I am here for having tried to put your father into prison.

Even then he might have escaped had not that eternally infamous pair of actors, Hawtrey and Brookfield, told Queensberry's lawyers where to look for evidence. And in order to secure a conviction the Crown had to promise immunity from prosecution to a series of blackmailers and male prostitutes.

After his release, Wilde described what English prisons were like at the time in two letters to the *Daily Chronicle* which cannot be read without tears and indignation; it is nice to learn that some of the reforms he proposed were presently adopted. In the latter part of his term he was fortunate to have a humane prison governor, Major Nelson, who allowed him writing materials, and he composed his epistle to Lord Alfred Douglas, which takes up eighty-seven pages in this volume. When, in 1905, Ross published less than half of it under the title "De Profundis," his intentions no doubt were good, but in fact he did Wilde a disservice, for the passages he selected are precisely those that are stylistically weakest and of dubious emotional honesty. When I read the book as a boy, I was revolted; it seemed awful to me that, under such terrible circumstances, a man could still write so stagily. Now, thanks to Mr. Hart-Davis, we have the whole definitive text, and it turns out to be a very different kind of document. (It appears that even the version based on a typescript which Wilde's son, Mr. Vyvyan Holland, published in 1949 was full of errors and omissions.)

Wilde on Jesus or redemption through suffering is as childish and boring as Gide on the same subjects, but Wilde on Bosie Douglas displays the insight, honesty, and unself-conscious style of a great writer. Their relationship is of the greatest psychological interest. It is clear that Wilde's infatuation for Bosie was not primarily a sexual one; one surmises that any sexual relations they may have had were infrequent and probably not very satisfactory. Bosie was leading a promiscuous life when they first met, he continued to lead it, and Wilde shows no signs of having been jealous. So far as sex was concerned, the main importance of Bosie in Wilde's life was that it was he who introduced Wilde, whose affairs had thitherto been confined to persons of his own class, to the world of male prostitution. When they met, Bosie, who was only just twenty-two, was already being blackmailed.

> Your defect was not that you knew so little about life, but that you knew too much. . . . The gutter and the things that live in it had begun to fascinate you. . . . terribly fascinating though the one topic round which your talk invariably centred was, still at the end it became quite monotonous to me.

Their mutual attraction—incapable of love as Bosie was, Wilde's existence was more important to him than the existence of anybody else except his father—was an affair of their egos rather than of their senses; one might say that the Overloved met the Underloved, and such an encounter is always extremely dangerous. Any child who discovers, as Bosie had, that he is hated and rejected by his father is bound to suffer from a feeling, however deeply he represses it, of profound unworthiness. If, when such a child grows up, he meets someone who appears to love him, particularly if this someone be older, his subconscious finds it impossible to believe that such a love is genuine, and he is driven, therefore, continually to test it by behaving badly. If the other rejects him, his suspicion is confirmed, but however often the other forgives, his suspicion can never be laid to rest for good and all. Further, if the feeling of unworthiness is strong enough, he may feel, again subconsciously, a contempt for anyone who offers him affection: if his father was right to reject him, then anyone who accepts him is a fool and deserves to be tormented. Wilde was a famous and successful author; the first test, therefore, was to find out whether his love for Bosie was stronger than his love of writing. Wilde's time had to be wasted:

> At twelve o'clock you drove up, and stayed smoking cigarettes and chattering till 1.30, when I had to take you out to luncheon at the Café Royal or the Berkeley. Luncheon with its *liqueurs* lasted usually till 3.30. For an hour you retired to White's. At tea-time you appeared again and stayed till it was time to dress for dinner. You dined with me either at the Savoy or at Tite Street. We did not separate as a rule till after midnight, as supper at Willis's had to wind up the entrancing day. That was my life for those three months, every single day, except during the four days when you went abroad.

Then, since the giving of money, particularly the giving of money for the primal childish pleasure of eating, is in our culture the symbol of all-giving love, Bosie had to see how much money he could get Wilde to spend on him:

> My ordinary expenses with you for an ordinary day in London— for luncheon, dinner, supper, amusements, hansoms and the rest of it—ranged from £12 to £20. . . . For our three months at Goring my expenses (rent of course included) were £1340. . . . My expenses for eight days in Paris for myself, you, and your Italian servant were nearly £150: Paillard alone absorbing £85.

Significantly, Bosie, on the ground that he would not give up their friendship, renounced his allowance from his father, and, on the ground that his mother's allowance was insufficient, refused to take money from her, but this did not mean that he was prepared to deny himself any luxuries; Wilde was to take the place of both of his parents as provider.

On the other hand, a child who, like Wilde, has been overloved and indulged by his mother, and who has discovered that he has the power to charm even those who are initially hostile, may consciously be vain but unconsciously feels insecure, for he cannot believe he is as lovable as his mother seems to think, and his power to charm others seems a trick that is no indication of his real value. When such a child grows up, his emotional involvements with others, especially if there is a sexual element present, are apt to be short-lived if the other succumbs to his charm without any resistance, but he can be fascinated by someone who, without rejecting him completely, treats him badly. If he is confronted with this novel experience, his very vanity is excited by the challenge of seeing how much he can endure, until enduring and forgiving become a habit.

> In every relation of life with others one has to find some *moyen de vivre*. In your case, one had either to give up to you or to give you up. . . . I gave up to you always. As a natural result, your claims, your efforts at domination, your exactions grew more and more unreasonable. . . . Knowing that by making a scene you could always have your way, it was but natural that you should proceed, almost unconsciously I have no doubt, to every excess of vulgar violence. . . . I had always thought that my giving up to you in small things meant nothing: that when a great moment arrived I could reassert my willpower in its natural superiority. It was not so. . . . My habit—due to indifference chiefly at first—of giving up to you in everything had become insensibly a real part of my nature. Without my knowing it, it had stereotyped my temperament to one permanent and fatal mood.

One cannot help speculating about what would have happened to their relationship if Queensberry had died; perhaps Bosie would simply have lost interest. As it was, his hatred of his father was the guiding passion of his life, so that Wilde as a person was less important to him than Wilde as a weapon, and subconsciously, maybe, Wilde and his father were symbolically interchangeable; it hardly mattered which went to prison so long as one of them did.

> When your father first began to attack me it was as your private friend, and in a private letter to you. . . . You insisted that the quarrel had nothing to do with me: that you would not allow your father to dictate to you in your private friendships: that it would be most unfair of me to interfere. You had already, before you saw me on the subject, sent your father a foolish and vulgar telegram. . . . That telegram conditioned the whole of your subsequent relations with your father, and consequently the whole of my life. . . . From pert telegrams to priggish lawyers' letters was a natural progress, and the result of your lawyer's letters to your father was, of course, to urge him on still further. You left him no option but to go on. . . . If his interest had flagged for a moment your letters and postcards would soon have quickened it to its ancient flame. They did so.

On one point only, I think, Wilde shows a lack of self-knowledge. He did, of course, realize exactly enough the folly he had committed in suing Queensberry:

> The one disgraceful, unpardonable, and to all time contemptible action of my life was my allowing myself to be forced into appealing to Society for help and protection against your father. . . . Once I had put into motion the forces of Society, Society turned on me and said, "Have you been living all this time in defiance of my laws, and do you now appeal to those laws for protection? . . . You shall abide by what you have appealed to."
> People thought it dreadful of me to have entertained at dinner the evil things of life, and to have found pleasure in their company. But they . . . were delightfully suggestive and stimulating. It was like feasting with panthers. . . . I don't feel at all ashamed of having known them. . . . Clibborn and Atkins were wonderful in their infamous war against life. To entertain them was an astounding adventure. . . . What is loathsome to me is the memory of interminable visits paid by me to the solicitor Humphreys in your company, when in the ghastly glare of a bleak room you and I would sit with serious faces telling serious lies to a bald man.

What Wilde failed to realize, however, was that, given the circumstances and his own character, he would sooner or later have had to take the action he did even if Bosie had not egged him on. If his card had been ignored, Queensberry would certainly have gone on to make louder accusations in even more public places, and a refusal by Wilde to answer them would have been taken by Society to mean that they were true; he would have escaped prison but not social ostracism. Some artists are indifferent to their social reputation; immersed in their work, they do not care which side of the tracks they are on. Had Verlaine received Queensberry's card, he would probably have written on it, *"Mais oui, je suis pédéraste,"* and sent it back. But for Wilde the approval of Society was essential to his self-esteem.

Bosie was a horror and responsible for Wilde's ruin, but if at the end of his life Wilde had been asked whether he regretted ever having met him, he would probably have answered no, and it would be presumptuous of us to regret it either. We cannot know what Wilde might have written if he had never met Bosie or had fallen in love with someone else; we can only note that during the four years between his meeting with Bosie and his downfall Wilde wrote the greater part of his literary work, including his one masterpiece. Perhaps Bosie had nothing to do with this, but perhaps he did, if only by forcing Wilde to earn money to support him.

The fact that, in spite of all he knew about him and everything which had happened, Wilde could write to Bosie, a few months after his release from prison:

> I feel that my only hope of again doing beautiful work in art is being with you. It was not so in the old days, but now it is different, and you can really recreate in me that energy and sense of joyous power on which art depends

and to Ross:

> Do let people know that my only hope of life or literary activity was in going back to the young man whom I loved

suggests that, despite the endless rows, the time-wasting and the expense, or even because of them, Bosie had served him as a Muse. Their reunion was unfruitful, to be sure, but by that time Wilde had lost the will to be inspired.

The post-prison letters are more interesting than the pre-prison. To begin with, Wilde is now a lonely man, without an audience of his social and intellectual equals, so he puts into his letters what in happier times he would have expressed in talk, and the reader gets glimpses of what his conversation must have been like:

> I assure you that the type-writing machine, when played with expression, is not more annoying than the piano when played by a sister or a near relation. Indeed many, among those most devoted to domesticity, prefer it.

> The sea and sky one opal, no horrid drawing-master's line between them, just one fishing boat, going slowly, and drawing the wind after it.

> Cows are very fond of being photographed, and, unlike architecture, don't move.

> The automobile was delightful, but, of course, it broke down: they, like all machines, are more wilful than animals—nervous, irritable, strange things: I am going to write an article on "nerves in the inorganic world."

... the Blessed St. Robert of Phillimore, Lover and Martyr—a saint known in *Hagiographia* for his extraordinary power, not in resisting, but in supplying temptations to others. This he did in the solitude of great cities, to which he retired at the comparatively early age of eight.

I believe they [the British public] would like me to edit prayers for those at sea, or to recant the gospel of the joy of life in a penny tract.

Wilde has some comic adventures. On the Riviera he meets a rich admirer, Harold Mellor, who treats him to champagne and invites him to Switzerland. Wilde accepts with joy and looks forward to living in the lap of luxury. But Switzerland is cold and damp, the boys are ugly, and Mellor turns out, like so many rich men, to be stingy; he serves only cheap Swiss wine and keeps his cigarettes locked up. In Paris, Wilde meets Morton Fullerton, an American journalist who had become bewitched by Henry James's prose style, and tries to borrow money from him. Fullerton refuses his request in the following words:

The maker of those masterpieces has too much delicacy and *esprit* not to sympathize sincerely with the regret of a man obliged to reply thus to an appeal which certainly he could not have expected, and for which it was impossible for him to prepare but which is none the less precious for that. I grope at the hope that meanwhile the stress has passed, and that you will not have occasion to put, *malgré vous,* either me or anyone else again into such a position of positive literal chagrin.

But as a whole these letters are, naturally, very sad reading—the record of a desperately unhappy man, who is going downhill and knows it. Other writers—Villon, Cervantes, Verlaine, for example —have suffered imprisonment (Villon even suffered torture), or, like Dante, suffered exile, without their creative powers being affected; indeed, they often wrote their best work after disaster. It was not his experiences in Reading Gaol, dreadful as these were, that put an end to Wilde's literary career, but the loss of social position. Another kind of writer might have found the disreputable bohemian existence to which, as an ex-convict, he was limited a relief—at least there was no need to keep up pretenses—but for Wilde the Bunburying, the double life, at one and the same time a bohemian in secret and in public the lion of respectable drawing rooms, had been the exciting thing, and when the drawing rooms withdrew their invitations he lost the will to live and write.

An artist by vocation may, like most men, be vain, desire immediate fame and fortune and suffer if they are withheld, but his vanity is always subordinate to his pride, which has no doubt whatever that what he writes is of unique importance. If, like Stendhal, he tells himself that he is writing for posterity, this is not, strictly speaking, true, since it is impossible to imagine what posterity will be like; it is his way of saying he is so convinced of the permanent value of his work that he is certain the world sooner or later will recognize it. He does not write to live, he lives to write, and what he enjoys or suffers outside the act of creation—his social and personal life—is to him of minor importance; no failure in either can diminish his confidence in his powers. Though he wrote one imperishable masterpiece, Wilde was not an artist by vocation but a performer. In all performers, vanity is stronger than pride, for a performer is truly himself only when he is in a sympathetic relation to an audience; alone, he does not know who he is. As Wilde said of himself:

> It is curious how vanity helps the successful man, and wrecks the failure. In old days half of my strength was my vanity.

So long as he was in prison and permitted to receive only a few letters, his knowledge of the outside world was confined to what his friends would tell him, and they, naturally, were anxious to cheer him up and refrained from dwelling on disagreeable facts. He did not realize either how poor he was going to be or how irrevocable was his loss of social position. Thus he can write hopefully, "I must live in England, if I am to be a dramatist again." The day after his release he visits his old friends the Leversons, and behaves, Mrs. Leverson records, as if nothing serious had happened:

> He came in with the dignity of a king returning from exile. He came in talking, laughing, smoking a cigarette, with waved hair and a flower in his button hole.

Ross adds:

> During that day and for many days afterwards he talked of nothing but Reading Prison and it had already become for him a sort of en-

chanted castle of which Major Nelson was the presiding fairy. The hideous machicolated turrets were already turned into minarets, the very warders into benevolent Mamelukes and we ourselves into Paladins welcoming Coeur de Lion after his captivity.

According to Ross, it took him five months before he fully realized that the Leversons' drawing room was not typical and that Society had neither forgotten nor forgiven and never would. For a vain man, his situation was appalling. Not only was he penniless and wholly dependent upon the charity of others but there was small possibility of his ever being able to earn his living again. Even if he had continued to write books and plays, no respectable publisher or producer would have dared print one or put one on the stage. He does manage to write one piece, "The Ballad of Reading Gaol," and hopes to get three hundred pounds for it from an American newspaper, but the highest offer made is one hundred, though he is offered a thousand for an interview. The only publisher he can find is Leonard Smithers, who has an ill name in the trade as a publisher of pornography, and when Smithers publishes "The Importance of Being Earnest," not one of the major English papers reviews it. Wilde's name is still "news" and where he goes and whom he sees is written up or invented by reporters, but in a very different way:

> I am in the Public Press sometimes "the ex-convict," which is too obvious: sometimes *"le poète-forçat,"* which I like, as it puts me in good company: sometimes I am "Mr. Oscar Wilde," a phrase I remember: sometimes "the man Wilde," a phrase I don't.

Social humiliation and insult are something he has to learn to expect:

> The middle-class English who are at the hotel have objected to my presence, and this morning I was presented with my bill and requested to leave by twelve o'clock. I declined to do this, and said I could not pay the bill today. They have given me till tomorrow at noon, and have asked me not to have my meals in the hotel.

> Yesterday I was by the sea and suddenly George Alexander appeared on a bicycle. He gave me a crooked, sickly smile, and hurried on without stopping.

> Cossie [Lennox] and Harry Melvill both cut me! I felt as if I had
> been cut by two Piccadilly renters. For people whom one has had to
> give themselves moral or social airs is childish. I was very much hurt.

A man who suffers an exceptional misfortune usually has another trial to bear. In addition to those who avoid him, since they
fear that misfortune, like influenza, may be infectious, there are
the professional pitiers who seek him out precisely *because* he is
unfortunate, and for a vain man the latter are probably the harder
to endure. Wilde does not mention meeting such persons himself,
but there is a remark in one of Ross's letters which suggests that he
did not escape their kind of attention.

To be financially dependent upon the charity of a wife whom he
had treated very badly would have been humiliating enough, but
the legal strings attached to his allowance were outrageous. Pay-
ment was to be withheld if, in the opinion of the solicitor, Wilde
was keeping disreputable company. Since nobody respectable would
speak to him, a literal obedience would have condemned him not
to speak to anybody. Ross courageously offered to come and live
with him but, with his characteristic decency, Wilde refused to let
Ross risk his reputation for his sake. He saw his friends whenever
they came to Paris, but most of the time he had nobody to talk to.
It is hardly surprising, therefore, that he turned to the only con-
solations readily available—drink and boys:

> I cannot bear being alone, and while the literary people are charm-
> ing when they meet me, we meet rarely. My companions are such as I
> can get, and I of course have to pay for such friendships. . . . To
> suggest I should have visitors of high social position is obvious, and
> the reason why I cannot have them is obvious also.

> How evil it is to buy Love, and how evil to sell it! And yet what
> purple hours one can snatch from that grey slowly-moving thing we
> call Time! . . . The Cloister or the Café—there is my future. I tried
> the Hearth, but it was a failure.

In France during the nineties, a single man could easily lead a
life of modest comfort on a hundred and fifty pounds a year, but
Wilde was incapable of living modestly. Besides social position, an
essential thing for him was, as Ross wrote, "contact with comely

things," meaning a certain standard of living—good food, drink, tobacco, clothes. Any deprivation of comfort threw him into a depression:

> A hole in the trousers may make one as melancholy as Hamlet, and out of bad boots a Timon may be made.

> Like dear St. Francis of Assisi I am wedded to Poverty: but in my case the marriage is not a success; I hate the bride that has been given me.

Not the least of the many merits of Mr. Hart-Davis's editing is that it finally disposes of a legend in which many, including myself, have believed—namely, that Wilde's last years were spent in abject poverty. From his own letters one might think so, for money—the lack of it, appeals for it, thanks for it, complaints that what is justly his has not been sent him, paranoid suspicions that he is being swindled—is an ever-recurring topic. There were certainly occasions when he found himself unable to pay essential bills—to hotels, for example—but nobody can be blamed for this except himself. The four months during which his wife stopped his allowance may have been difficult; otherwise, it was paid and continued to be paid after her death, and it was by no means his only source of income. Lady Queensberry sent him money regularly, his friends sent him checks whenever they could, and there were assuredly givers whose names we do not know. Where money was concerned, he became sly and untruthful, like an alcoholic; he sold the option on an idea for a play, finally written by Frank Harris under the title "Mr. and Mrs. Daventry," to six different people. Ross, who had known him in the old days, and knew, therefore, what Wilde meant by "a certain standard of living," says categorically, "This, since his release, he *was able to have* except for a few weeks at a time, or perhaps months." Of Wilde's income during the last eleven months of his life, Ross states:

> To *my* knowledge since January last he had £400 over and above the annuity of £150 paid from his wife's trustees through me—£300 came from the Queensberry family and £100 from a theatrical manager, while his expenses in Italy were all paid by a Mr. Mellor who was travelling with him and has always been most kind to him.

There are so many sad and grievous circumstances in his later career, that there is no necessity for those who were interested in him to be harrowed by imaginary pictures of his poverty.

How did he get through what was, in those days, quite a considerable sum? It is not hard to guess that little of it was spent on necessities like food and lodging, and a good deal on drink, on boys who "bayed for boots," and, most likely, too, on overgenerous gifts to beggars and excessive tips, for a person who, like Wilde, has loved playing the role of a king distributing largess finds it impossible to abandon even when he has lost his throne and the purse is no longer his.

The tape recorder is not my favorite instrument. In the old days only God heard every idle word; today it is not only broadcast to thousands of the living but also preserved to gratify the idle curiosity of the unborn. But this invention does allow full justice to be done to the great performer; Malibran is merely a name in operatic history, yet our great-grandchildren will be able to pass their personal judgment upon Flagstad and Callas. Malibran, at least, did nothing but sing; we easily believe that she was a great singer because all her contemporaries thought so and we have no evidence that might lead us to doubt their taste. But suppose she had also been a second-rate composer whose music had been greatly overestimated by her contemporaries; we should then inevitably wonder whether their taste in singing was any more reliable than their taste in music. It is impossible for us to be just to Wilde because, although his contemporaries all agreed that his improvised conversation was superior to his writings, they also thought the latter much better than we do. Of his poems not one has survived, for he was totally lacking in a poetic voice of his own; what he wrote was an imitation of poetry-in-general. His prose letters to the *Daily Chronicle* about prison life are authentic, "The Ballad of Reading Gaol" is not; reading such stanzas as the following, the reader would never guess that their author had been in prison himself, only that he had read "The Ancient Mariner":

> They glided past, they glided fast,
>   Like travellers through a mist:

> They mocked the moon in a rigadoon
> Of delicate turn and twist,
> And with formal pace and loathsome grace
> The phantoms kept their tryst.
>
> With mop and mow, we saw them go,
> Slim shadows hand in hand:
> About, about, in ghostly rout
> They trod a saraband:
> And the damned grotesques made arabesques,
> Like the wind upon the sand!

Of his nondramatic prose, we can still read "The Happy Prince and Other Tales" with great pleasure, and "The Soul of Man Under Socialism" and "Intentions," for all their affectation, contain valuable criticism, but "The Portrait of Mr. W. H." is shy-making and "The Picture of Dorian Gray" a bore.

His development as a dramatist is interesting. Both in England and in France, even the most talented playwrights of the day were bewitched by a conception of drama that was sterile and self-frustrating—one that Shaw correctly diagnosed as an attempt to produce a genus of opera without music:

> The drama can do little to delight the senses: all the apparent instances to the contrary are instances of the personal fascination of the performers. The drama of pure feeling is no longer in the hands of the playwright: it has been conquered by the musician.

The typical fashionable play of the period was a melodramatic libretto *manqué*; indeed, a number of plays, including "Salomé," which have long since vanished from the theatre, are flourishing to this day in the opera house. Shaw's conclusion, which was valid for himself, was that the future of drama without music lay in the drama of thought. Wilde could not have taken the Shavian path because he was not a thinker; he was, however, a verbal musician of the first order. While "Salomé" could become a successful libretto, "Lady Windermere's Fan," "A Woman of No Importance," and "An Ideal Husband" could not, because their best and most original elements—the epigrams and comic nonsense—are not settable; at the same time, their melodramatic operatic plots spoil them as spoken drama. But in "The Importance of Being Earnest," Wilde

136   W. H. Auden

succeeded—almost, it would seem, by accident, for he never realized
its infinite superiority to all his other plays—in writing what is perhaps the only pure verbal opera in English. The solution that,
deliberately or accidentally, he found was to subordinate every
other dramatic element to dialogue for its own sake and create a
verbal universe in which the characters are determined by the kinds
of things they say, and the plot is nothing but a succession of opportunities to say them. Like all works of art, it drew its sustenance
from life, and, speaking for myself, whenever I see or read the play
I always wish I did not know what I do about Wilde's life at the
time he was writing it—that when, for instance, John Worthing
talks of going Bunburying, I did not immediately visualize Alfred
Taylor's establishment. On rereading it after his release, Wilde
said, "It was extraordinary reading the play over. How I used to toy
with that Tiger Life." At its conclusion, I find myself imagining a
sort of nightmare Pantomime Transformation Scene in which, at
the touch of the magician's wand, instead of the workaday world's
turning into fairyland, the country house in a never-never Hertford-
shire turns into the Old Bailey, the features of Lady Bracknell into
those of Mr. Justice Wills. Still, it is a masterpiece, and on account
of it Wilde will always enjoy the impersonal fame of an artist as
well as the notoriety of his personal legend.

For many years, both in England and in America, the Wilde
scandal had a disastrous influence, not upon writers and artists
themselves but upon the attitude of the general public toward the
arts, since it allowed the philistine man to identify himself with the
decent man. Though the feeling that it is sissy for a boy to take an
interest in the arts has probably always existed among the middle
class and is not yet extinct, for many years after Wilde's trial it was
enormously intensified. In fairness to the middle class, however,
one must admit that such a feeling is not totally without justification. The artist and the homosexual are both characterized by a
greater-than-normal element of narcissism, though neither has as
much as the performing *artiste;* it is only likely that among artists
and *artistes* as a class a higher-than-average per cent will also be
homosexual, compared with many other professions. Again, while
the prudery and self-righteousness of the middle class in the nine-

teenth century were repellent traits, we must not romanticize either the working class or the aristocracy of the period because of their relative tolerance; the working-class husband beat up his wife when drunk, the aristocrat regarded sexual exploitation of the poor as his natural right. Had Wilde been an aristocrat, his class brothers would have seen to it that there was no public scandal; since he was a person of middle-class origin who had pushed his way into high society, they left him to his fate with, perhaps, a certain feeling of satisfaction at the downfall of someone who had risen above his proper station.

In the long run, I think one may say that the effect of what in itself was a horrid business has been beneficial. Today, nearly seventy years later, both the working class and the aristocracy in the nineteenth-century sense have disappeared and we live in a middle-class society, but one which has learned that the problem not of homosexuality only but of sexual life in general cannot be solved by pretending it does not exist. If we have learned to listen to what Freud and others tell us about the complicated role which sexuality plays in our lives and the dubious character of violent moral indignation at the sexual behavior of our neighbor, if, indeed, we are now able to read these letters without prurient interest as we would read the letters of anybody else who wrote entertaining ones, Wilde has certainly helped us to do so.

Christ and Wilde

by G. Wilson Knight

. . . I do not claim to know the exact degree of Wilde's legal guilt. He himself said that "while there was much amongst the definite charges that was quite untrue" his life had certainly "been full of perverse pleasures" (*De Profundis, The Works of Oscar Wilde,* ed. G. F. Maine, 1948 etc.; 883). The nature of his relationship to his mother is said to have left him with what psychologists call a "mother fixation" (Frank Brennand, *Oscar Wilde,* 1960; I. 15); the association recalls Byron's, though Byron's was less happy. His mother dressed him as a girl until he was nine (Brennand, I. 15). Like Byron, Wilde was a lover of children (*Lord Byron: Christian Virtues,* II. 75–83; Hesketh Pearson, *The Life of Oscar Wilde,* Penguin 1960 edn., XI. 187; XVII. 334), and both exerted a strong fascination over women. Both often appeared effeminate, and yet both were capable, when challenged, of disconcerting feats of male strength. Wilde's love of flowers and interest in both male and female dress—he started his literary career as editor of a woman's periodical—were allied with a robust physique, physical courage, intellectual brilliance and a devastating wit to give him a position of artistic and social dominance that proved intoxicating both to others and to himself. From youth onwards he maintained, like Byron, a boyish immaturity often difficult to distinguish from the integration of a seer.

Within was a strong idealism and a rich mine of human sympathy. His first play *Vera or the Nihilists* sets a justified revolution against a tyrannic aristocracy and touches solution under the crown—"this little fiery-coloured world" (IV)—an enlightened sovereign, and love; through these, unified and expanded, is glimpsed a solution to human misery. *Vera* is of a higher order than his subsequent dramas; it failed; but its key-thoughts continued to impregnate Wilde's serious writing. *The Soul of Man under Socialism* demonstrates the necessity of preserving the individual's freedom or soul-worth within our planning; seeing the royal, or aristocratic, valuations *as they exist in each one of us,* as sacred. The symbol of this soul-worth may be the crown; or more often riches, and especially jewels. Jewels and other rich solids constitute Wilde's central symbolism; for him the City of God is "like a perfect pearl" and "the pearl of my soul" a natural phrase (*De Profundis*; *Works*; 865, 866).

Throughout literature rich metals are used ambivalently.[1] They may hold connotations of material greed or may be symbols of the transcendent. Jewels normally exert positive radiations. The Kingdom of Heaven is a "pearl" and the New Jerusalem made of precious stones (*Matthew*, XIII. 46; *Revelation*, XXI. 18–21). Dante's *Divina Commedia* sparkles, and Milton's *Paradise Lost* is loaded, with rich stones. We have Shakespeare's "mine eternal jewel" for the soul in *Macbeth* (III. i. 68), Othello's "pearl" as a love-symbol (V. ii. 346) and the jewel-imagery in *Pericles* (III. ii. 102; and see *The Shakespearian Tempest,* V. 222–3; also II. 65–9); Byron's contrast of "seraph"-eyed Aurora and Haidée in terms respectively of a jewel-like transcendence and flowery nature in *Don Juan* (XV. 45, 47, 58; XVI. 48); Yeats' metal-imagery and Gold Birds in *Sailing to Byzantium*; and the spiritualized gems at the conclusion of Sir Herbert Read's *The Green Child*. We may compare Charles Doughty's beautiful passage on gems in his *Travels in Arabia Deserta* (edn. of 1926; XI. 315): "Those indestructible elect bodies, as stars, shining to us out of the dim mass of matter, are comfortable to our fluxuous feeble souls and bodies; in this sense all gems are cordial and of an influence religious. These elemental flowering lights almost persuade us of a serene eternity." "Flowering"; and

---

[1] This ambivalence is discussed in my article "*Timon of Athens* and its Dramatic Descendants," *The Review of English Literature,* II. iii; Oct., 1961.

yet rich metals contrast with flowers in point of solidity. In them spirituality is solid and beauty permanent: even a miser's lust has a transcendental aspect.

Rich metals are apt correlatives to transcendence housed in male beauty. In the love-duologue of the *Song of Solomon* the female receives her best adulation in imagery of fertility (p. 212), the male in imagery of rich stones. His fingers are like "golden tapers" tipped with "topaz," his body "ivory" veined with "sapphire" and his limbs of "marble" and "gold" (V. 10–15). This supposedly physical description blends readily with a vision of the seraphic, as recorded by Daniel:

> . . . I saw a man standing, robed in linen, with a girdle of fine gold from Ophir round his waist, his body gleaming like a topaz, his face like lightning, his eyes like lamps of fire, his arms and legs like the colour of burnished bronze, and the sound of his words like the noise of a crowd!   (*Daniel*, X. 5)

Such elaborated metallic associations would not be quite so suitable for a woman. We are reminded of the Oriental phrase "diamond body" (Norman O. Brown, noting Rilke's poetic quest for the hermaphroditic, *Life against Death*, 1959; XVI. 313), used to designate the etheric, or astral, body which interpenetrates and survives the physical.

Wilde as aesthete knew both the fascination and the danger of the transcendent housed in the material. Through young male beauty he saw an eternal, jewel-like, perfection. But his experience of it, as of rich stones too, was ambivalent, balanced between eye-lust and transcendence. Almost lust was transcendence; or rather the lust aroused was *a lust for the transcendent*. This was Wilde's star; it, like the Crown in *Vera*, should somehow, if joined to love, be the heart of a great good: a Christian good. The complexities are handled in his parables.

In *The Young King* a prince before his coronation dreams of those who suffer to make his luxury and state, and accordingly rejects his coronation finery for a beggar's clothes. Standing before the image of Christ he prays and is transfigured:

> And lo! through the painted windows came the sunlight streaming upon him, and the sunbeams wove round him a tissued robe that was

fairer than the robe that had been fashioned for his pleasure. The
dead staff blossomed, and bare lilies that were whiter than pearls.
The dry thorn blossomed, and bare roses that were redder than rubies.
Whiter than fine pearls were the lilies, and their stems were of bright
silver. Redder than male rubies were the roses, and their leaves were
of beaten gold.

The flowering metals point a merging of nature into the transcendent. The "Glory of God" fills the church and as the Young
King comes from the altar "no man dared look upon his face, for
it was like the face of an angel."

Variations are played on the central theme. Our next hero, in
The Fisherman and his Soul, gives up his soul, which henceforth
exists without a "heart," for love of a Mermaid, the Soul returning
to tempt him to crime with lures of gold and luxury. Here natural
love and nature, with water and flowers as fertility symbols, are on
the one side and the soul, crime, and riches are on the other.
Riches, even when evil, are to be aligned with the "soul"—a key-
concept in Wilde—here functioning as tempter. Easier alignments
occur in *The Star-Child*, where a star-born child becomes a boy of
beauty and Narcissistic pride, scorning poverty and ugliness and
engaging in deliberate cruelty. Punished by the loss of his beauty
and now himself an outcast, from the depths of his suffering he
takes pity on a diseased beggar; so winning back his beauty and
being finally crowned as a king.

Wilde is trying to relate his central intuition of youthful beauty
to love and good works. That a kind of love-wisdom rather than any
normal love is his true centre can be seen indirectly from the contrast of a natural and flower-like love with the soul in *The Fisherman and his Soul*. Wilde senses a dangerous co-presence of selfishness and spirituality, an all-too-solid presence of a transcendency
directly associated with the "soul," and yet seemingly as *infertile as
rich gems;* and as dangerous. How, then, may the "soul" and its
jewelled and seemingly infertile Eros be related to love and Christian values? Young royal figures help most, since their human
beauty lives and acts within the temporal order under the Crown
whose rich stones symbolize the eternal.

In *The Happy Prince* the aim is clearer: the parable expresses
the potential sovereignty of youth-beauty or love-wisdom even

though, in our era, it is constricted. The Happy Prince is a gilded
city-statue with sapphires for eyes and a ruby on his sword-hilt,
much admired for his beauty and like an "angel." He is a royal
Eros. A Swallow, symbolizing the human self, leaves his lady, a
Reed, because of her feminine ways, and rests beneath the statue,
which is weeping for human misery. Being himself fixed, the Prince
needs the Swallow for three missions, and sends him bearing his
ruby and two sapphires in turn to a destitute mother and her fever-
struck little boy; to a young author cold and starving; and to a little
girl, seller of matches, in dire need. Finally he gets the Swallow to
strip the gold-leaf from his body piece by piece to relieve the destitute within the city. The Happy Prince symbolizes *that within the
erotic vision which is not being used;* recalling to our minds those
stores of "hidden kindness and power" in man of which Nietzsche
speaks (*Thus Spake Zarathustra,* 55). Though set on high where he
can *see* "all the ugliness" and "all the misery" of mankind, yet he
himself "cannot move"; but though his heart is of "lead," his beauty
has the needed wealth; and after he is melted down and only his
leaden heart survives with the dead Swallow, God in his good time
will welcome both to his "garden of Paradise" and "city of gold."
Every phrase is loaded. It is a consummate and final statement,
even to the heart of lead. Though the emotion may be, or seem,
worthless, it survives the fires of mortality.

The essence of love-wisdom is creativity. Plato's final doctrine in
The Symposium defines it as the desire to "beget upon the thing of
beauty" (206); having glimpsed the transcendent and creative essence within the youth-bud more excelling than maturity, to make
from this sight fine works in art or action (209). In two sonnets
(113, 114; *The Mutual Flame,* I. v. 119–20) Shakespeare tells how
the harmony seen in his Fair Youth is next seen everywhere, in all
that is most deformed and ugly; Nietzsche speaks of "the creative
friend that hath ever a perfect world in his gift" (*Thus Spake
Zarathustra,* 16); and Robert Bridges of "our happiest earthly com-
panionships" as holding a foretaste of (i) "salvation" and (ii) some
"super-humanity" to be (*The Testament of Beauty,* IV. 1408–11).
So too Christian love may be defined as the love "for the ideal of
man in each individual" and to generate this love the admiration

of *one* individual may be enough (Sir J. R. Seeley, *Ecce Homo*, 1865; XIV). Such is the doctrine within *The Happy Prince*: Eros, weeping for sympathy with human misery, wants the human soul to spend his wealth.

Difficulties remain. The beauty, unlike female beauty, is, as Shakespeare's Sonnets drive home (e.g. Sonnet 104), though a window into the eternal, yet in earthly terms transient; and so is the purity, or virtue, which it appears, for a while, to express. In *The Picture of Dorian Gray* the young hero of amazing beauty becomes, like the Star-Child, cruel and vicious, and though he remains outwardly young and perfect his advancing age and crimes are horribly objectified in the ever-changing and damning portrait, which recalls the externalized evil of *The Fisherman and his Soul*. What is the relation of human beauty to worth? Do we admire form and colour only, or do we in the act of adoration see through to the soul, as Spenser in his *Hymn in Honour of Beauty* (120–140) and *Epithalamion* (186) thought? Is human beauty simply in Byron's phrase "the precious porcelain of human clay"? Or shall we, looking inwards, compare it to "a lighted alabaster vase"? (*Don Juan*, IV. 11; VIII. 96). May not the soul-flame, when tested, prove ugly? Is there nothing both exquisite and permanent, except jewels, which are anyway infertile unless on a crowned king? *Dorian Gray* contains one of Wilde's finest passages on jewels (XI); and it is surely the subtlest critique of the Platonic Eros ever penned. Throughout Wilde's thought-adventures there is this analysis of the interrelationship of soul, beauty and Christian goodness. Somehow there must be a harmony and a permanence and a creative result. But how? Perhaps the truth can only be tragically defined; and perhaps, from the depths, he realized this.

Not only was Wilde's a quest of a high order, but it had strong Christ-like affinities. The New Testament wavelength and Biblical style of the Parables is obvious; and from his youth onwards Wilde was deeply attracted, and in his works again and again engaged, by the Christian religion. In *Salome* a decadent and bejewelled paganism in a sulphurous atmosphere of beauty and blood-lust asserts itself statically and repetitively against the equally repetitive denunciations of Jokanaan, or John the Baptist, whom Salome de-

sires. Always in Wilde the two worlds want to meet. Here they co-
exist in unhealthy opposition: the atmosphere is like pressure before
thunder.

We must see Wilde's homosexual engagements in the context of
these works. They were prompted by his innate love of all youth
from children upwards and also by his own state of male-female,
and often seemingly boy-like, integration. The drama of his relationship to Lord Alfred Douglas, with its see-saw of idealisms and
angers, repeats the story of those Sonnets of Shakespeare of which
Wilde has himself left us a study in *The Portrait of Mr. W. H.*,
relating the Fair Youth to the boy-girl actors of Shakespeare's stage.
Wilde's less idealistic engagements were prompted by (i) the instinct, as felt by Shakespeare, Byron and Nietzsche, to plunge low
when the disparity between the near-integrated self and the community becomes unbearable . . . so that we find him writing,
"Tired of being on the heights, I deliberately went to the depths
in the search for new sensation" (*De Profundis*; *Works*, 857); and
(ii) by a genuine liking for the lower orders of society; not any deep
and lasting love for any one person, but a lightning contact with
thrill in the very disparity and sexual ratification of human unity.
He once said that he found the young men of the underworld as
dangerously fascinating as "panthers" (*De Profundis*; *Works*, 882).

And because there is an exhibitionist compulsion on such men
to reveal themselves, Wilde could not remain content with his
social mask. Though he was genuinely fascinated by the glitter of
high society which was, like his jewels, a symbol of his aim, he also
saw through the superficiality, making his terms with it, like Hamlet
and Byron, by wit. That could not last; his scornful speech of
congratulation to his first-night audience for admiring one of his
comedies was in part genuine, the more so since he must have
known that the play was inadequate. So, as though compelled by
an instinct for self-revelation, he half-willingly exposed his life
to society's revulsion. He played with fire, "with that tiger, Life"
(Pearson, XIV. 255), in deadly earnest, and when he might have
done so refused, again and again, to escape the conflagration.
"That," he said, "would be a backward step" (Pearson, XV. 276).
This does not mean that he did not suffer, but simply that he was
impelled from the depths to put in train and abide by a sequence

of events which would lead to suffering. As Lewis Broad puts it, "the vision of St. Sebastian, 'the youngest of the martyrs,' had vividly impressed him, years before" (*The Truth about Oscar Wilde*; 1957 edn.; XV. 175). Such men may appear to embrace their martyrdom—"I had to pass on" (*De Profundis*; *Works*, 866) —but it remains a martyrdom, a crucifixion, a self-exhibition in agony and shame. The shame may be of the essence; at the least it shatters all the pseudo-dignities and masks of our lying civilization.

At his trial Wilde also lied in answer, though he might have done better to speak out. And yet he did, on the important issue, speak firmly. The famous letter of his to Lord Alfred Douglas containing the phrase "your slim-gilt soul that walks between passion and poetry" may appear over-decorative, but the words are precise. "Slim-gilt," if we remember *The Happy Prince*, Wilde's jewel-symbolism and the term "diamond body" for the etheric or spirit body interpenetrating the physical . . . , is an exact term for the seraphic intuition. "Between passion and poetry" matches the blend of instinct and intellect within the Platonic Eros. Of this blend Lord Alfred Douglas had been the symbol, the living truth. Faced with this letter and the words in Lord Alfred's sonnet on "the love that dare not speak its name," Wilde replied:

> The "love that dare not speak its name" in this century is such a great affection of an elder for a younger man as there was between David and Jonathan, such as Plato made the very basis of his philosophy, and such as you find in the sonnets of Michelangelo and Shakespeare.

He continued by asserting its "spiritual" nature and its relation to "works of art"; its worth as "the noblest form of affection"; its natural quality and its intellectual status. According to Lewis Broad this defence has been called "the finest speech of an accused man since that of Paul before Agrippa" (Broad, XIV. 167; *Acts*, XXVI).

Wilde's *De Profundis*, written from prison, is a commentary, from a Nietzschean standpoint, on his tragic experience. Sorrow and suffering are now experienced as revelations of the creative purpose; the wholeness of his own drama is accepted and ratified; the deep insights of his parables, which he recalls, are lived. There is no repentance, no morality in any usual sense, but there is a lengthy and profound concentration on Christ. From the start Christian sympathies had run concurrently with his Hellenic and aesthetic passions. Now Christ is his central interest. He is seen as, above all, the supreme artist; more, as the first and greatest romantic, behind the romances of medievalism, of Shakespeare, and of more modern times. He notes his respect, so like Wilde's own— as indeed he himself says (*De Profundis*; *Works*; 875)—for children as exemplars for us all; and his insistence on wholeness, recalling how he himself had written in *The Soul of Man under Socialism* "that he who would lead a Christ-like life must be entirely and absolutely himself" (*Works*, 867). Christ had a strange sympathy with sinners:

> The world had always loved the saint as being the nearest possible approach to the perfection of God. Christ, through some divine instinct in him, seems to have always loved the sinner as being the nearest possible approach to the perfection of man . . . To turn an interesting thief into a tedious honest man was not his aim . . . The conversion of a publican into a Pharisee would not have seemed to him a great achievement. But in a manner not yet understood of the world he regarded sin and suffering as being in themselves beautiful holy things and modes of perfection.
>
> (*Works*, 877)

Wilde admits the danger, and also agrees on the need for some kind of repentance, viewed in Shakespearian wise (*The Sovereign Flower*, V. 249) simply as *recognition*, in order to harmonize and ratify the whole (877–8). He is trying to see life-as-art, with tragic form. More precisely, he is asserting, in the manner of Browning's *The Statue and the Bust*, that within the criminal there may exist certain elements of fire and courage necessary to perfection but too often absent from morality. He is thinking less of any sin of his own—he himself regrets nothing (866)—than of the fascination exerted on him by the young "panthers" and "gilded snakes," whose "poison was part of their perfection" (882), of the underworld. His main emphasis on Christ's repudiation of legality and hypocrisy is valid, and his relation of Christ's Judaea to his own Britain (876) reasonable. The essay is written from a Nietzschean standpoint recognizing that "between the famous and the infamous there is but one step, if as much as one" (862).

Christ is a key to Wilde's life. I quote again from Hesketh Pearson. Wilde was "drawn to the personality of Jesus Christ" (XI. 188) and his interest "increased every year until at length he almost identified himself with Christ and often spoke in parables" (X. 141). "Both thought and taught in stories, and both had a strong intuition of their tragic destiny" (XIII. 218). One of his parables, *The Doer of Good*, was on Christ (XIII. 218; *Works*, 843). "He saw himself in the role of Christ, the shouts of his first-night audiences being his hosannas," with Calvary to follow (XV. 282). He felt that his life needed a tragic completion (XV. 282) and wooed disaster "under the influence of a mystical concept" (XV. 284). While there was still time to flee, "He has resolved," said his brother, "to stay, to face it out, to stand the music like Christ" (XV. 301). Finally "his own condemnation and sufferings had completed the parallel with Jesus which for many years he had instinctively drawn" (XVI. 323); and "in his last years the two figures whom Wilde was readiest to talk about were Napoleon and Jesus Christ" (XVIII. 358).

Those who knew Wilde personally recognized a stature impossible to recapture from reported epigram and printed essay. Beerbohm Tree's comment is typical: "Oscar was the greatest man I have ever known—and the greatest gentleman" (Pearson, XIV. 232). His record of lived virtue recalls Byron's, though he lacked Byron's thrust and range of purpose. The softer intuitions of both were on the wavelength of Christ's. Resemblances to Christ are clear in Wilde's Byronic love of children, his egotism blended with humility, his repartee, his utter lack of malice, his forgiveness and Timon-like generosity (e.g. Pearson, XVII. 335); his magnanimity, his refusal to save himself, and patient endurance of shame. His record of kindly actions is as high as Byron's (e.g. Pearson, V. 65; VI. 73); his fight for removing the hideous wrongs of children in prison alone (*Letter to the Daily Chronicle, Works*; 897–903), when set against the system, leaves no question as to Wilde's moral superiority over the society that condemned him. Long before his own fall, he had like Christ a natural sympathy with all outcasts (Pearson, VII. 93–4). His natural friendliness for the rough and low from his American tour onwards is recorded again and again. Active criminals were rapidly deflected by his courteous and kindly reception (Pearson, XV. 273; XVIII. 367) and what he wrote of Christ was true of himself: "He does not really teach one anything, but by being brought into his presence one becomes something" (*De Profundis*; *Works*, 878). Naturally, he made friends in prison. A warder, named Martin, at Reading gaol wrote of him: "What that poet was before he went to prison I care not. What he may have been after he left prison I know not. One thing I know, however, that while in prison he lived the life of a saint, or as near that holy state as poor mortal can ever hope to attain" (Broad, XVII. 193). Vincent O'Sullivan received the same impression: "If terrible sufferings courageously borne, the enduring of dire injustice and reviling without complaint, be matter of saintliness, then Wilde was a saint" (Pearson, XVIII. 358).

How far the analogy to Christ is valid we cannot say without a much deeper knowledge of the forces in play than we at present possess; and it would be wise to suspend judgement. Honesty at least will not deny that it would have been our loss had Wilde's life been other than it was. This is not to say that his actions were right, but rather that to us his actions together with their consequences are extraordinarily valuable; they are at least tragically justified.[2] His story dramatizes much that lies close to the essence of art. His statement that "the artist must live the complete life, must accept it as it comes and stands like an angel before him, with its drawn and two-edged sword" (Pearson, XVIII. 357)—"angel" to match the homosexual-seraphic and "two-edged" to cover tragedy— is *not* true of the artist; but it may be true of those who attempt the yet higher and far more difficult quest of living their art. Wilde's most famous works were written for money, and are of the second order only; and his paradoxes, on paper, pall. His genius went into his life, his living talk; into his spoken or written parables; and into *Dorian Gray*, itself an extended parable. He was by instinct a teacher. When his last days are called "unproductive," Hesketh Pearson justly comments, "Yet no one has ever called Christ or Socrates unproductive because each of these spoke his thoughts instead of writing them down" (XVIII. 366); and each, like Wilde, uncomplainingly paid the penalty demanded by civilization for their impact.

---

[2] This is perhaps a place to pay a tribute to the fine film based on John Furnell's vivid dramatization of Wilde's life, *The Stringed Lute*.

Wilde's life is a drama, and seen in all its excess, its brilliance, its degradation and its tragedy, it has the form needed to correspond to the matters contained. His flamboyance, exhibitionism and heady enjoyment of success, these must be admitted; and also his shocking inability—Timon-like in this as in his generosity—to handle money (Pearson, XVIII. 363), his dishonest misleading of his legal helpers, and his unjust attack on Lord Alfred Douglas written from prison. But all must be judged in relation to the difficulties inherent in his life's central, Blakean, aim: to make of the senses elements of a new spirituality, to cure the soul by the senses and the senses by the soul (*The Picture of Dorian Gray*, II: *Works*, 29, 31). This aim he carried through with a daring consistency; it motivated alike his aestheticism, his anti-social acts and his perception of Christ. About his lowest engagements there was an element of the sacramental. Of cruelty he knew as little as he knew of caution; his instincts were of a childlike, positive and embracing kind. In these terms he lived and acted in allegiance to the royalty of the crowned and diamonded Eros. His sin was total self-expression acted out in spontaneity "not wisely but too well"; and he took tragedy uncomplainingly in his stride.

His influence for good, though it was an influence that cold print cannot record, was empowered by a Falstaffian and Byronic humour (e.g. Pearson, quoting Douglas, XVIII. 359; also 367). According to *Thus Spake Zarathustra* our new, Renaissance, way beyond religion must include humour, without which "truth" is suspect (56), for "all good things laugh" (73). "I have hallowed laughter" (73) means the hallowing of much before which religion veils its eyes. Powys in *Rabelais* (1948; Part IV) explains this new life-wisdom. Wilde went far to incarnate it.

The Social Rebel

by George Woodcock

Wilde's only social tract is *The Soul of Man Under Socialism*, but before that pamphlet was written he had already included in *The Critic as Artist* a number of comments on political matters which indicated the general tendency of his social thought and showed the consistency of his libertarian views.

In the latter work he contends that it is impossible for the politician or the social reformer preoccupied with narrow issues to view objectively the realities of social life. "The necessity of a career," as he says, "forces everyone to take sides."

He then goes on to criticise the mere reformism, by which the socially minded of his age strove to delay a social reorganisation based on entirely new conceptions of justice and morality.

> We are trying at present to stave off the coming crisis, the coming revolution as my friends the Fabianists call it, by means of doles and alms. Well, when the revolution or crisis arrives, we shall be powerless, because we shall know nothing. . . . What we want are unpractical people who see beyond the moment, and think beyond the day. Those who try to lead the people can only do so by following the mob. It is through the voice of one crying in the wilderness that the ways of the gods must be prepared.

He proceeds to attack the general attitude of the philanthropists who try to change or improve man from without. It is only by developing himself, he states, that a man can be of any use, either to himself or to others.

> For the development of the race depends on the development of the individual, and where self-culture has ceased to be the ideal, the

intellectual standard is instantly lowered, and, often, ultimately lost. . . . The real weakness of England lies, not in incomplete armaments or unfortified coasts, not in the poverty that creeps through sunless lanes, or the drunkenness that brawls in loathsome courts, but simply in the fact that her ideas are emotional and not intellectual.

Here is individualist philosophic anarchism of the purest kind, and this theory is expanded and applied to direct social issues in *The Soul of Man Under Socialism.*

This pamphlet cannot be called a really great work, either of literature or of social thought. From a literary point of view it is more sprawling and unpolished than the rest of Wilde's essays. From a social point of view it is sketchy and derivative. On the other hand, it has real virtues, since Wilde's epigrammatic style enables him to convey, in a phrase, a social judgment which a more ponderous thinker might have needed a chapter to build up by solemn argument. His pamphlet also, in its very haste, gives a feeling of sincerity which we do not always gain from his more elaborately finished works.

His plea for Socialism begins on an individualist basis, since he sees the virtue of a social reorganisation in the fact that it "would relieve us from that sordid necessity of living for others which, in the present condition of things, presses so hardly upon almost everybody."

Altruism, Wilde contends, leads more often to the perpetuation of social distress than to its elimination. It neither helps the philanthropist nor his subject, and usually results merely in keeping the poor alive in their misery. "The proper aim is to try to construct society on such a basis that poverty will be impossible, and the altruistic virtues have really prevented the carrying out of this aim." In fact, charity, far from helping the poor, merely demoralises them.

"Under Socialism," says Wilde, "all this will be altered." But he is very careful to define his meaning of socialism in such a way that it is quite clearly understood to mean libertarian and not authoritarian socialism.

Socialism, Communism, or whatever one chooses to call it, by converting private property into public wealth, and substituting co-operation for competition, will restore society to its proper condition of a thoroughly healthy organism, and ensure the material well-being of each member of the community. It will, in fact, give Life its proper basis and its proper environment. But, for the full development of Life to its highest mode of perfection, something more is needed. What is needed is Individualism. If the Socialism is Authoritarian; if there are Governments armed with economic power as they are now with political power; if, in a word, we are to have Industrial Tyrannies, then, the last state of man will be worse than the first.

Wilde demands for every man the rights of individual development which up to now only a few scholars and artists have enjoyed. He sees that though in some cases property has allowed individual development, in general it is an institution that corrupts and burdens both the rich and the poor. On the so-called "virtues of the poor" he is particularly eloquent and acute. The best of the poor, he contends, far from being grateful for charity, are "ungrateful, discontented, and rebellious." In this they are quite right, for it would be merely brutal to remain contented with a low mode of life. "Disobedience . . . is man's original virtue. It is through disobedience that progress has been made, through disobedience and through rebellion." Similarly, the poor man who practices thrift is wrong: he should refuse to live "like a badly fed animal" and "should either steal or go on the rates." And Wilde concludes that:

> I can quite understand a man accepting laws that protect private property, and admit of its accumulation as long as he himself is able under those conditions to realise some form of beautiful and intellectual life. But it is almost incredible to me how a man whose life is marred and made hideous by such laws can possibly acquiesce in their continuance.

Wilde goes on to praise the work of agitators who show the poor how they should really live and thus help to provoke social upheavals. Thence he returns to his insistence on the need for a libertarian conception of socialism, since the poor cannot be freed by subjecting the whole community to compulsion.

> Every man must be left quite free to choose his own work. No form of compulsion must be exercised over him. If there is, his work will not be good for him, will not be good in itself, and will not be good for others. And by work I simply mean activity of any kind. . . . All association must be quite voluntary. It is only in voluntary associations that man is fine.

It is then argued that, while private property has enabled individualism to exist, it has not been the right kind of individualism. For property has perverted individualism by making gain its aim rather than growth. It has made men forget that the true perfection does not lie in having, but in being. It has stultified the individualism of the poor by starving them, and that of the rich by burdening them with possessions.

> What a man really has, is what is in him. What is outside of him should be a matter of no importance.
> With the abolition of private property, then, we shall have true, beautiful, healthy Individualism. Nobody will waste his time in accumulating things, and the symbols for things. One will live. To live is the rarest thing in the world. Most people exist, that is all.

Later in his essay, Wilde mounts an open attack on the very idea of government, and shows, as thoroughly as Godwin, how every form of government carries its evil within. Despotism, oligarchy, democracy are all shown to have their own faults. All authority, indeed, is degrading, to those who use it as well as to its victims. Authority violently abused has the single virtue that it provokes revolt; authority exercised kindly, by means of rewards, is wholly demoralising to all it affects.

From a condemnation of government, Wilde goes on to an equally anarchistic condemnation of punishment:

> As one reads history . . . one is absolutely sickened, not by the crimes which the wicked have committed, but by the punishments which the good have inflicted; and a community is infinitely more brutalised by the habitual employment of punishment, than it is by the occasional occurrence of crime. . . . Starvation, and not sin, is the parent of modern crime. . . . When private property is abolished, there will be no necessity for crime, no demand for it; it will cease to exist. Of course, all crimes are not crimes against property. . . . But though a crime may not be against property, it may spring from the misery and rage and depression produced by our wrong system of property-holding, and so, when the system is abolished, will disappear. When each member of the community has sufficient for his wants, and is not interfered with by his neighbour, it will not be an object of any interest to him to interfere with anyone else.

This attitude to crime is all the more interesting, since at the time when he wrote *The Soul of Man Under Socialism* Wilde can have had little reason to suppose that circumstances would make him one of the most celebrated among the "criminal classes." It is foreshadowed in his essay on Wainwright, and, naturally enough, it was to find more than an echo in his writings after his own imprisonment among the people whom society chooses to isolate and punish as "criminals."

Wilde sees government replaced by a "State" that will in fact have very little similarity with the institution usually understood by such a term, since he says that it is not to govern, and defines it as "a voluntary association that will organise labour, and be the manufacturer and distributor of necessary commodities."

He has no anti-mechanistic illusions of the dignity of manual labour. Indeed, he sees dull and monotonous labour as degrading, and recognises the function of machinery as a liberator of man from the great mass of such necessary but frustrating toil.

> Is this Utopian? A map of the world that does not include Utopia is not worth even glancing at, for it leaves out the one country at which Humanity is always landing. And when Humanity lands there, it looks out, and, seeing a better country, sets sail. Progress is the realisation of Utopias.

Wilde continues with an elaborate discussion of the application of individualism to art, which is perhaps too long for the balance of his essay. Then he returns in quite definite terms to his revolutionary conclusion, a conclusion which is in complete accord with his manifestations of sympathy towards anarchists, criminals and other social rebels.

> Man has sought to live intensely, fully, perfectly. When he can do so without exercising restraint over others, or suffering it ever, and his activities are all pleasurable to him, he will be saner, healthier, more civilised, more himself. Pleasure is nature's test, her sign of approval. When man is happy, he is *in* harmony with himself and his environment.

This essay represented Wilde's real social beliefs. Some of his biographers have tried to show that it was merely the result of a passing enthusiasm inspired by hearing Shaw's lecture on Socialism.

But in fact, as Hesketh Pearson has pointed out, "his whole trend of thought was antagonistic to the Webb-Shavian deification of the state," and there is no doubt that *The Soul of Man* really did mirror Wilde's personal discontent with society as he found it, and gave a picture of the kind of world in which he would like men to live.

This pamphlet has never been regarded as important in the English Socialist movement, perhaps because it was so much in opposition to the dominant tendencies, but it had much popularity abroad. If Sherard is to be believed, millions of copies were sold in Central and Eastern Europe, and it gained a great reputation among the discontented classes under the Russian, German and Austrian despotisms of the period. In America large pirated editions were printed and sold by revolutionary groups. In England its most important immediate result was to create feeling against Wilde among the influential and moneyed classes.

In the heyday of Wilde's success, from the writing of *The Picture of Dorian Gray* to his abrupt fall from popularity, he seemed rather to turn away from his social ideals. The success of his plays, with their fabulous earnings, turned his head, and there is no doubt that for a period of at least two years he lived very selfishly, and that then the worst sides of his character came to the surface in arrogance and inconsiderate self-indulgence.

Yet even at this period his writings contain a powerful element of social criticism. The English upper-classes represented in his plays are caricatured with clear hostility, and Wilde does not hesitate to pillory their corruption, their shallowness, their snobbery, their lack of genuine moral scruples. Here and there, too, he inserts epigrams which show his contempt for their social attitude. In both *The Picture of Dorian Gray* and *A Woman of No Importance*, there appears a statement which reproduces one of the main contentions of *The Soul of Man Under Socialism*. The conversation turns to the problem of the East End. A politician remarks that it is "a very important problem," and the wit (Lord Henry Wotton in the novel and Lord Illingworth in the play) replies: "Quite so. It is the problem of slavery. And we are trying to solve it by amusing the slaves."

A Woman of No Importance has, indeed, a general atmosphere of social protest, not only in the satirical and bitter (as far as Wilde was capable of acrimony) attitude towards the upper-classes, but also in the main plot, which is clearly built around a social problem, already sketched in *Lady Windermere's Fan*, of the inequality of men and women in modern society and the ruthlessness of the conventional social code towards the individual who, deliberately or unwillingly, acts against its arbitrary laws. The theme is partly imbued with that sentimentality which in a character like Wilde's always underlies his more obvious cynicism, but this quality is made less obvious by the sparkling wit with which the dialogue flits lightly over the whole range of social life and the political scene. The theme is presented conventionally, in the differing lives of Lord Illingworth, the successful and ruthless public figure, into whose witty conversation Wilde put much of himself, and Mrs. Arbuthnot, by whom Illingworth had a child many years before. The son of this transitory union, grown into an intelligent youth, attracts Illingworth's interest, so far that he proposes to take him as a secretary. In this way are shown the contrasting fates of the man and the woman: Lord Illingworth, who goes through life gaily and unscathed by his cynical refusal to protect the mother of his child from the hostility of conventional society by marrying her, Mrs. Arbuthnot, enduring a life of lonely guilt and bitterness and now faced by the last humiliation of seeing her son wish to go away with the man who has been the cause of her own lifelong misery. The wicked lord is finally defeated when, for a wager with the equally wicked Mrs. Allonby, he attempts to kiss the prudish young American girl, Hester Worsley, with whom his son is in love. The boy turns against him, and Illingworth, his belated paternal feelings defeated, turns tail and departs, after an unpleasant scene with Mrs. Arbuthnot.

Undoubtedly, in his treatment of this plot, Wilde was largely motivated by a desire to give the Victorians a rather sentimental theme of the kind to which they were accustomed, as a means of transmitting the brilliant verbal wit which was always the most pleasant ingredient of his plays—to the author even more than to the audience. Nevertheless, the particular choice of a plot is always significant, and I have no doubt that Wilde, who edited an intellectual woman's paper for some years, and who often had a high opinion of the capacities of the women he encountered in literary society, deliberately intended to draw attention to sexual equality of rights. I think it is also reasonable to assume that, like most cynics, Wilde had a strongly humane aspect to his character, which appears often in his works; *The Ballad of Reading Gaol* is one example, while in parts of *De Profundis* this quality is shown, almost, at times, to the extent of sentimental atrocity.

Nevertheless, however conventionally conceived may have been the main feminist plot of *A Woman of No Importance,* it is presented with great wit and much reason. Wilde's conclusions can best be summarised in a sound remark he made elsewhere, that he was against the existence of one law for men and one for women, and would prefer to see no law for anybody.

This play also contains a quite severe attack on the contemporary British upper-class. There are many bitter social epigrams, and in one place the American girl, Hester Worsley, becomes the mouthpiece for a really scathing condemnation. Although it is spoken by a character towards whom Wilde might at first seem unsympathetic because of her militant puritanism, this tirade nevertheless appears to represent his own real views on these people for whom, while he was attracted towards the richness of their lives like a moth to the fatal candle, he felt a very great contempt. Among a group of superficial upper-class women, Hester bursts out into this tirade:

> You rich people in England, you don't know how you are living. How could you know? You shut out from your society the gentle and the good. You laugh at the simple and the pure. Living, as you all do, on others and by them, you sneer at self-sacrifice, and if you throw bread to the poor, it is merely to keep them quiet for a season. With all your pomp and wealth and art you don't know how to live—you don't even know that. You have the beauty that you can see and handle, the beauty that you can destroy, and do destroy, but of the unseen beauty of life, of the unseen beauty of a higher life, you know nothing. You have lost life's secret.

The next play, *An Ideal Husband,* represents an even more open attack on the social system, in that its basic theme is the innate corruption of political life. A politician, Sir Robert Chiltern, has begun his career by selling State secrets to an international financier, and from the money he has gained by this initial corruption, rises to the heights of a political career. When he reaches this position, his past is used as a means of blackmail by a woman who wishes him to support a fraudulent canal scheme, and thus assure the success of its promoters. He is saved from this threat, not by his virtues, but by his friend, Lord Goring, applying counter-trickery to Mrs. Cheveley, the blackmailer. In a circle where all are guilty, Chiltern, who has gained most by his roguery, is able to escape without punishment, and the height of his career is reached in a hypocritical speech wherein he denounces "the whole system of modern political finance," regardless of the fact that he is one of the worst examples of its use. His duplicity gains him universal praise for integrity, and so the political farce is drawn to its usual end.

Wilde has been criticised for not bringing a just retribution to the contemptible Chiltern. But in fact he does not accept the justice of Chiltern's fortune; he merely records the fact that in political life fraud and hypocrisy always win the prizes.

In this connection it should be remarked that Wilde showed a consistently hostile attitude towards politics and politicians, not only in his writings, but also in his personal life. There were those among his friends who regretted that, with his gift for talking, he did not go into parliamentary life; one of these was Yeats who, with his odd idea that Wilde was by nature a man of action, said to O'Sullivan: "He might have had a career like that of Beaconsfield, whose early style resembles his, being meant for crowds, for excitement, for hurried decisions, for immediate triumphs." Anything less calculated for crowd appeal than Wilde's conversational or literary style it is difficult to imagine, and when Oscar was told of the idea that he was a man of action, he remarked, disparagingly, "It is interesting to hear Yeats' opinion about one."

According to Douglas, he professed to be a Liberal, but he mocked the Liberals as much as the Tories, and Douglas thought that he never showed enough interest in either party to vote in an election. When his political friends, admiring his conversational gifts, tried to persuade him to accept a safe seat in Parliament, he turned down the offer without hesitation. He admired Disraeli as a man and a writer, but appeared to regret that he should have spoilt himself by going into politics.

O'Sullivan has said that the main ideas of Wilde's plays are few and simple, and describes them thus: "He disliked hypocrisy in social intercourse, he glorified individualism, he denied the moral right of the community to sacrifice the life of any member of it." But, in *An Ideal Husband* at least, we must add his strongly critical attitude towards political life, which occurs in many quite deliberate statements of opinion in various parts of the play.

For instance, when Robert Chiltern is trying to prepare his wife for a revelation of his predicament, which he knows will shatter the pedestalled ideal she has always made of him, he says to her:

> Gertrude, truth is a very complex thing, and politics is a very complex business. There are wheels within wheels. One may be under certain obligations to people that one must pay. Sooner or later in political life one has to compromise. Everyone does.

Then there is the even more revealing conversation between Chiltern and Goring, in which Chiltern tells how he was corrupted by Arnheim with his philosophy of power. Goring, who acts in this play as Wilde's personal voice, expresses his complete disagreement with this philosophy.

> *Chiltern.* One night after dinner at Lord Radley's the Baron began talking about success in modern life as something that one could reduce to an absolutely definite science. With that wonderfully fascinating quiet voice of his he expounded to us the most terrible of all philosophies, the philosophy of power . . . that power—power over other men, power over the world—was the one thing worth having, the one supreme pleasure worth knowing, the one joy one never tired of, and that in our century only the rich possessed it.
>
> *Goring (with great deliberation).* A thoroughly shallow creed.
>
> *Chiltern (rising).* I didn't think so then. I don't think so now. Wealth has given me enormous power. It gave me at the very outset of my life freedom, and freedom is everything. You have never been poor, and never known what ambition is. You cannot understand what a wonderful chance the Baron gave me. Such a chance as few men get.
>
> *Lord Goring.* Fortunately for them, if one is to judge by results.

This attitude towards politics and the political life is supported by a whole series of epigrams scattered throughout the play. An example is Goring's remark to his father: "My dear father, only people who look dull ever get into the House of Commons, and only people who are dull ever succeed there."

The Importance of Being Earnest stands alone among Wilde's plays in having no explicit social theme, but even that play contains, in Lady Bracknell, a satire on the snobbish values of the upper-classes, while Miss Prism and Doctor Chasuble represent respectively Wilde's contempt for the educational system and the Church of his day.

There are some who have tried to elevate Wilde's homosexual practices and his three trials into a great act of rebellion against society. But here is an evident distortion, for all his actions during this period show the weaker side of his character, and reveal him as the victim rather than the defiant rebel.

To begin, Wilde's homosexual activities, however one may support his liberty to practise them and condemn the monstrous laws that inflicted on him such a terrible punishment, represented nothing particularly revolutionary. Homosexual practices, if not so openly recognised and tolerated as they are to-day, were very widespread in London, and it is said that during the 1890's no less than 20,000 people in that city alone were known to the police for this reason. But the police then, as now, turned as blind an eye as possible to such activities, and did not prosecute homosexuals unless they committed some really flagrant indiscretion which brought their case into publicity.

Wilde was for long so discreet, and so far from drawing public attention to his concealed life, that until the time of his trials many of his intimate friends, including Sherard and Frank Harris, were completely unaware that he had been a practising pederast for nearly a decade. It was only fellow homosexuals like Ross and Reggie Turner who knew this side of his life, and they concealed it in their own interests. His fear of exposure led him into furtive relationships with a despicable set of male prostitutes who were afterwards willing to be cajoled and bribed into betraying him to the law, and, however Wilde may later have dramatised his "sins," they remain a rather sordid story, in which the one really rebellious character is Taylor, the procurer who refused to give evidence against Wilde and chose instead to stand in the dock beside him and share his imprisonment.

Wilde's action against Queensberry was also that of a discreet man who wished to *appear* to conform, and it contained a dishonesty which did not fit his declared attitude of social defiance. For Queensberry's accusation that Wilde *posed* as a "sodomite" [*sic*] was in fact short of reality. Wilde sued Queensberry in the hope of scotching the rumours that were growing up round his activities, so that he might continue them in more security, and he was also propelled into this course by Alfred Douglas's antagonism towards his father. It is clearly ridiculous to suggest that there was anything of the great rebel in going to law with a man who had said about him something less than the truth, merely in order to preserve a false appearance in the eyes of society. Wilde was hoist on his own petard; the fate he had desired to impose on Queensberry was meted out to him, and in his later days he would have been the last to deny that he had only his own folly and inconsistency to thank for his downfall. In *De Profundis* he commented on the poetic justice of his fate:

> The one disgraceful, unpardonable, and to all time contemptible action of my life was to allow myself to appeal to society for help and protection. To have made such an appeal would have been from the individualist point of view bad enough, but what excuse can there ever be put forward for having made it? Of course once I had put into motion the forces of society, society turned on me and said, "Have you been living all this time in defiance of my laws, and do you now appeal to these laws for protection? You shall have these laws exercised to the full. You shall abide by what you have appealed to." The result is I am in gaol. Certainly no man ever fell so ignobly, and by such ignoble instruments, as I did.

Once Wilde realised he was caught in the toils of a hostile law, he began to fight back and show defiance. There was his famous duel of wit with Carson, and, later, his impassioned defence of love between men from the dock of the Old Bailey, when he cried out:

> The "love that dare not speak its name" in this century is such a great affection of an elder for a younger man as there was between David and Jonathan, such as Plato made the very basis of his philosophy, and such as you will find in the sonnets of Michael Angelo and Shakespeare. It is that deep, spiritual affection which is as pure as it is perfect. It dictates and pervades great works of art like those of Shakespeare and Michael Angelo, and these two letters of mine, such as they are. It is in this century misunderstood, so much misunderstood

that it may be described as the "love that dare not speak its name," and on account of it I am placed where I am now. It is beautiful, it is fine, it is the noblest form of affection. There is nothing unnatural about it. It is intellectual, and it repeatedly exists between an elder and a younger man, when the elder man has intellect, and the younger man has all the joy, hope, and glamour of life before him. That it should be so the world does not understand. The world mocks at it, and sometimes puts one in the pillory for it.

But the value of such defiance was largely vitiated by the fact that it was used in defence of an untruth. Of course, there is no cause to blame Wilde for denying the charges against him when he was faced with a thoroughly savage and immoral law, but the fact remains that he did not practise the defiance of a rebel, who would have admitted what was attributed to him, and defended himself by attacking the law.

Nor should it be forgotten that Wilde's decision to stay and face his ruin was hardly motivated by any idea of rebellion, but partly by the pressure of his family, with their foolish ideas of the duties of an Irish gentleman, and partly by that very strongly fatalistic feeling which we have already noticed as prominent in his philosophy, and which undoubtedly helped his decision to drift with the rapids of destiny once he was caught in their tow.

Yet, while in this whole affair Wilde was motivated by no truly rebellious impulse, his acts unconsciously produced an important social effect, since the publicity given to homosexuality and the indignation of all thinking men at home and, even more so, abroad, at the savagery of his sentence, resulted in a gradual but profound change in the public attitude towards this particular sexual eccentricity. As Laurence Housman has said:

> Always, so long as it stays remembered, the name of Oscar Wilde is likely to carry with it a shadowy implication of that pathological trouble which caused his downfall. And whatever else may be said for or against the life of promiscuous indulgence he appears to have led, his downfall did at least this great service to humanity, that, by the sheer force of notoriety, it made "the unmentionable" mentionable.

Prison broadened Wilde's social outlook in two important ways: firstly, by bringing him into close and equal contact with working-class people, and, secondly, by revealing to him in concrete form the kind of atrocities which society is always prepared to wreak on those who break the moral and criminal codes which are regarded as necessary for its existence. In this condemnation of all the worst evils of an authoritarian society he became more than ever convinced of the need for a change that would humanise social relationships and remove the fearful cruelties always associated with the domination of man by man.

For a number of reasons, including Wilde's own mental condition at the time, and the requirements of the prison regulations, it was the first of these discoveries that appeared most strongly in *De Profundis*, where he expressed something of his appreciation of the kindness and solidarity he found among the poor towards those who were victims of society and its harsh laws.

> The poor are wise, more charitable, more kind, more sensitive than we are. In their eyes prison is a tragedy in a man's life, a casualty, something that calls for sympathy in others. They speak of one who is in prison as of one who is "in trouble" simply. It is the phrase they always use, and the expression has the perfect wisdom of love in it.

Wilde was impressed and pleased at the contrast between this attitude of working-people and that of his literary and upper-class friends, who, with very few exceptions, regarded him as a pariah from the day his action against Queensberry failed. After he left Reading Gaol, he often spoke with affection of the men he had met in prison, and maintained a correspondence with some of the prisoners and the more friendly warders, a few of whom visited him in his exile near Dieppe. He even went so far as to provide cash out of his own scanty means, so that those he knew to be needy should not come out of prison in complete destitution.

His condemnation of the system that had tortured him and his fellow prisoners was the dominant theme of the only literary works of any importance which he produced during the last phase of his life. These are *The Ballad of Reading Gaol* and the two letters which he wrote to the *Daily Chronicle* on prison conditions soon after his release from gaol.

The first of these letters appeared on May 28th, 1897, and was prompted by the news that Warder Martin, a man who by his repeated kindnesses had helped to soften the last few months of

Wilde's imprisonment, had been dismissed from the service for the crime of giving a few biscuits to a hungry child.

In Wilde's day, children were still imprisoned in the ordinary gaols, and this happened even when they were merely on remand. Wilde was profoundly disturbed by the sufferings he saw inflicted on these terrified young boys.

He begins with an attack on the stupidity of the system whose unconscious cruelty produces such evil and brutal results, and returns to his old criticism of the faults inherent in any type of authority.

> It is the result in our own days of stereotyped systems, of hard-and-fast rules, and of stupidity. Wherever there is centralisation there is stupidity. What is inhuman in modern life is officialdom. Authority is as destructive to those who exercise it as it is to those on whom it is exercised. It is the Prison Board, and the system that it carries out, that is the primary source of the cruelty that is exercised on a child in prison.

Wilde then describes in detail what a child endures in prison— the hardships he shares with other inmates, but which react with peculiar severity on his unformed and easily disturbed nature. He ends by saying that, if a child is corrupted by prison life, it is due, not to the prisoners, but to—

> . . . the whole prison system . . . the governor, the chaplain, the warders, the solitary cell, the isolation, the revolting food, the rules of the Prison Commissioners, the mode of discipline, as it is termed, of the life.

He adds some equally pungent remarks on the prison treatment of the mentally unbalanced, describing in detail one particularly shocking case of the persistent punishment of a madman which he had witnessed during his own imprisonment and which had caused him great unhappiness.

His letter aroused much attention, and, if Frank Harris is to be believed, it had some effect in procuring a mitigation of the conditions under which children were imprisoned.

The second letter was occasioned by a proposal of the Home Secretary to reform the prison system by appointing more inspectors. Wilde points out that this would do more harm than good, since the evils of prison life were caused largely by the prison regulations, and it would only make matters worse if the code were more rigorously observed. He adds:

> The necessary reforms are very simple. They concern the needs of the body and the needs of the mind of each unfortunate prisoner.

With regard to the first, there are three permanent punishments authorised by law in English prisons:

1. Hunger.
2. Insomnia.
3. Disease.

He describes in some detail the bad and unhealthy food given in the prisons (food more appallingly inadequate even than that of a modern English prison), the foul sanitary arrangements, the insomnia caused by the barbaric sleeping facilities, the monotonous toil which takes its toll on weak and poorly fed bodies, the illnesses that arise from these abundant contributory causes, and the unjust and unimaginative punishment inflicted on any prisoner who, from weakness or incapacity, fails to fulfill all the requirements of this brutal system.

Nor are the mental consequences of imprisonment, he goes on to show, any less terrible, for deprivation of books and human intercourse brutalise the prisoner and drive him into a mentally unbalanced condition.

But even the reform of these abuses would not be enough without a change in the character of the prison staff. It would be necessary to "humanise the governors of prisons, to civilise the warders, and to Christianise the Chaplains."

This second letter, also, was received with much more friendly interest than might have been expected, and it seems possible that Wilde's protests helped to prepare the very inadequate reforms which have since taken place in the English penal system.

There remained one terrible feature of the penal system, the punishment of hanging, and Wilde's protest against this social enormity formed the main theme of the last and greatest of his poems, *The*

Ballad of Reading Gaol, into which he condensed all the bitterness and pity engendered by his own prison life, and all of his renewed sense of indignation at social injustice.

The Ballad of Reading Gaol, as well as being the best and most original of Wilde's own poems, is also one of the few permanently successful propaganda poems written in the English language, an ironical fact when one considers that Wilde has been regarded, and usually regarded himself, as the high-priest of Art for Art's sake. At times it sinks into a rather banal sentimentality, but often it has a bare strength which is quite unlike anything else in Wilde's works.

The poem tells of the execution of a young soldier during Wilde's confinement in Reading Gaol. The story is immaterial; what is important is the way in which Wilde conveys the horror of judicial murder and the dreadful character of the life which prisoners live. There is a unique and terrible intensity in such passages as this, in which, after his famous remark that—

> *Each man kills the thing he loves,*
> *Yet each man does not die,*

he goes on to show those terrors which the common man cannot share with the condemned murderer:

> *He does not feel that sickening thirst*
> *That sands one's throat, before*
> *The hangman with his gardener's gloves*
> *Comes through the padded door,*
> *And binds one with three leathern thongs,*
> *That the throat may thirst no more.*
>
> *He does not bend his head to hear*
> *The Burial Office read,*
> *Nor, while the anguish of his soul*
> *Tells him he is not dead,*
> *Cross his own coffin, as he moves*
> *Into the hideous shed.*

The poem is filled with passages showing equally strongly how Wilde came to identify himself imaginatively with the man who was suffering. Nor are there lacking vivid sketches of the misery to which he and his fellows who endured only a living and temporary death were condemned.

> *We tore the tarry rope to shreds*
>   *With blunt and bleeding nails;*
> *We rubbed the doors, and scrubbed the floors,*
>   *And cleaned the shining rails:*
> *And, rank by rank, we soaped the plank,*
>   *And clattered with the pails.*
> *We sewed the sacks, we broke the stones,*
>   *We turned the dusty drill:*
> *We banged the tins, and bawled the hymns,*
>   *And sweated on the mill,*
> *But in the heart of every man*
>   *Terror was lying still.*

And so the poem continues, in a great Jeremiad of indignation and lamentation, a veritable cry from the heart of despair which is quite unlike anything else that Wilde ever wrote in its fevered outpourings of mingled pity and anger, until he reaches his great indictment of the whole system of which prison is the extreme representation:

> *I know not whether Laws be right,*
>   *Or whether Laws be wrong;*
> *All that we know who lie in gaol*
>   *Is that the wall is strong;*
> *And that each day is like a year,*
>   *A year whose days are long.*
>
> *But this I know, that every Law*
>   *That men have made for Man,*
> *Since first Man took his brother's life,*
>   *And the sad world began,*
> *But straws the wheat and saves the chaff*
>   *With a most evil fan.*
>
> *This too I know—and wise it were*
>   *If each could know the same—*
> *That every prison that men build*
>   *Is built with bricks of shame,*
> *And bound with bars lest Christ should see*
>   *How men their brothers maim.*

Since Wilde's day, two great wars have given two generations of intellectuals some chance to see the inside of prisons as conscientious objectors. But none among them has yet written any attack on the prison system, either in prose or verse, that is quite so damning as *The Ballad of Reading Gaol*. With all its literary faults, it remains unique in the history of penological literature. If Wilde had produced nothing ese, this poem alone would have justified him as a writer.

Thus, the last of Wilde's writing was a work in which the whole theme was one of humane protest, and this is not out of keeping with the current of his development. As I have shown, he was much more acutely conscious of the ills of society than his critics would like us to believe. Certainly, his sense of social criticism was far more highly developed than that of the great majority of his literary contemporaries. He believed always and fervently in the intrinsic value of the individual; he denied the right of society to condemn any of its members to misery, or to warp their lives by its demands. He hated authority, cruelty, ugliness, in life as in art. He saw clearly the evils inherent in the twin systems of property and government. He detested oppression and injustice, and would always defend the downtrodden and persecuted. Beneath all his superficial callousness, he was a great humanist, and made the freedom of individual men the first article of his social creed. Wherever else he may have seemed insincere, in these matters he always spoke with a conviction that cannot be held in doubt.

Wilde and Nietzsche

by *Thomas Mann*

We must not forget that Nietzsche's moral criticism is to some extent impersonal, an attribute of his era. For around the turn of the century the European intelligentsia was making its first head-on assault upon the hypocritical morality of the middle-class Victorian age. Nietzsche's furious war against morality fits to a considerable extent into the general picture, and there is often a surprising family resemblance between his onslaughts and those of others. It is certainly a surprise to observe the close kinship of many of Nietzsche's *aperçus* with the far from vain tilts against morality with which, at approximately the same time, Oscar Wilde was shocking and amusing his public. When Wilde declares: "For, try as we may, we cannot get behind the appearance of things to reality. And the terrible reason may be that there is no reality in things apart from their experiences"; when he speaks of the "truth of masks" and the "decay of the lie"; when he bursts out: "To me beauty is the wonder of wonders. It is only shallow people who do not judge by appearances. The true mystery of the world is the visible, not the invisible"; when he calls truth something so personal that the same truth can never be recognized by two different minds; when he says: "Every impulse that we strive to strangle broods in the mind and poisons us. . . . The only way to get rid of a temptation is to yield to it"; and: "Don't be led astray into the paths of virtue!"— we cannot help seeing that all these quotations might have come from Nietzsche. And when, on the other hand, we find Nietzsche

"Wilde and Nietzsche" (Editor's title). From "Nietzsche's Philosophy in the Light of Recent History," in *Last Essays* by Thomas Mann, trans. Richard and Clara Winston and Tania and James Stern (New York: Alfred A. Knopf, Inc., 1958; London: Martin Secker & Warburg, Ltd., 1959), pp. 157–58, 172. © Copyright 1958 by Alfred A. Knopf, Inc. Reprinted by permission of Alfred A. Knopf, Inc., and Martin Secker & Warburg, Ltd.

saying: "Earnestness, that unmistakable sign of slow metabolism"; or: "In art lies are hallowed and the will to deception has a clear conscience on its side"; or: "We are basically inclined to maintain that the falsest judgments are the most indispensable to us"; or: "It is only moral prejudice to assert that truth is more valuable than appearance"—there is not one of these sentences which could not have occurred in Wilde's comedies and have earned a laugh in the St. James's Theatre. Those critics who ranked Wilde high compared his plays with Sheridan's *The School for Scandal.* Much that Nietzsche wrote seems to have come out of this school.

Of course there is something almost sacrilegious about the juxtaposition of Nietzsche and Wilde, for the latter was a dandy, the German philosopher a kind of saint of immoralism. And yet the more or less sought-after martyrdom at the end of Wilde's life— Reading Gaol—adds to his dandyism a touch of sanctity which would have aroused Nietzsche's full sympathy. What reconciled Nietzsche ultimately to Socrates was the end, the cup of hemlock. He held that this martyr's death had made an inestimable impression upon Greek youth and upon Plato. Similarly, he excepted the person of Jesus of Nazareth from his hatred for historical Christianity, again on account of the end, the crucifixion which he loved to the depths of his being, and to which he himself willingly submitted. . . .

A revision is due in the theory that Nietzsche was a writer of aphorisms without any central core to his thinking. His philosophy is quite as much a thoroughly organized system as Schopenhauer's. It evolves out of a single fundamental idea which pervades the whole of it. But this starting-point is, it must be granted, of a starkly aesthetic sort—which in itself would place his vision and thought in irreconcilable opposition to all socialist doctrine. In the final analysis there are only two basic attitudes, two points of view: the aesthetic and the moral. Socialism is a strictly moral worldview. Nietzsche, on the other hand, is the most uncompromisingly perfect aesthete in the history of thought. His major premise, which contains within itself his Dionysiac pessimism—namely, that life can be justified only as an aesthetic phenomenon—applies exactly to himself, to his life, his thinking, and his writing. These can be justified, understood, honored, only as an aesthetic phenomenon.

Consciously, down to his self-mythologizing in his last moment, down to madness, this life was an artistic production, not only in terms of its wonderful expressiveness, but in terms of its innermost nature. It was a lyric, tragic spectacle, and one of utmost fascination.

It is curious, although comprehensible, that aestheticism was the first manifestation of the European mind's rebellion against the whole morality of the bourgeois age. Not for nothing have I coupled the names of Nietzsche and Wilde—they belong together as rebels, rebels in the name of beauty, for all that the German iconoclast's rebellion went tremendously deeper and cost tremendously more in suffering, renunciation, and self-conquest. . . .

About Oscar Wilde

by Jorge Luis Borges

To mention Wilde's name is to mention a dandy who was also a poet; it is to evoke the image of a gentleman dedicated to the paltry aim of startling people by his cravats and his metaphors. It is also to evoke the notion of art as a select or secret game—like the work of Hugh Vereker and Stefan George—and the poet as an industrious *monstrorum artifex* (Pliny, XXVIII, 2). It is to evoke the weary twilight of the nineteenth century and the oppressive pomp one associates with a conservatory or a masquerade ball. None of these evocations is false, but I maintain that they all correspond to partial truths and contradict, or overlook, well-known facts.

For example, consider the notion that Wilde was a kind of symbolist. A great many facts support it: around 1881 Wilde directed the Aesthetes and ten years later, the Decadents; Rebecca West falsely accused him (*Henry James*, III) of imposing the stamp of the middle class on the Decadents; the vocabulary of the poem "The Sphinx" is studiously magnificent; Wilde was a friend of Schwob and of Mallarmé. But one important fact refutes this notion: in verse or in prose Wilde's syntax is always very simple. Of the many British writers, none is so accessible to foreigners. Readers who are incapable of deciphering a paragraph by Kipling or a stanza by William Morris begin and end *Lady Windermere's Fan* on the same afternoon. Wilde's metrical system is spontaneous or simulates spontaneity; his work does not include a single experimental verse, like this solid and wise Alexandrine by Lionel Johnson:

> Alone with Christ, desolate else, left by mankind.

Wilde's technical insignificance can be an argument in favor of his intrinsic greatness. If his work corresponded to the sort of reputation he had, it would consist merely of artifices like *Les Palais Nomades* or *Los crepúsculos del jardín*, which abound in Wilde— remember Chapter XI of *Dorian Gray* or "The Harlot's House" or "Symphony in Yellow"—but his use of adjectives gave him a certain notoriety. Wilde can dispense with those purple patches—a phrase attributed to him by Ricketts and Hesketh Pearson, but which had already appeared elsewhere earlier. The fact that it was attributed to Wilde confirms the custom of linking his name to decorative passages.

Reading and rereading Wilde through the years, I notice something that his panegyrists do not seem to have even suspected: the provable and elementary fact that Wilde is almost always right. *The Soul of Man under Socialism* is not only eloquent; it is just. The miscellaneous notes that he lavished on the *Pall Mall Gazette* and the *Speaker* are filled with perspicuous observations that exceed the optimum possibilities of Leslie Stephen or Saintsbury. Wilde has been accused of practicing a kind of combinatorial art, in the manner of Raymond Lully; that is perhaps true of some of his jokes ("one of those British faces that, once seen, are always forgotten"), but not of the belief that music reveals to us an unknown and perhaps real past (*The Critic as Artist*), or that all men kill the thing they love (*The Ballad of Reading Gaol*), or that to be repentant for an act is to modify the past (*De Profundis*), or that (and this is a belief not unworthy of Léon Bloy or Swedenborg) there is no man who is not, at each moment, what he has been and what he will be (*ibid.*).[1] I do not say this to encourage my readers to venerate Wilde; but rather to indicate a mentality that is quite unlike the one generally attributed to Wilde. If I am not mistaken, he was much more than an Irish Moréas; he was a man of the eighteenth century who sometimes condescended to play the game of symbolism. Like Gibbon, like Johnson, like Voltaire, he was an ingenious man who was also right. He was "remarkable for the

[1] Compare the curious thesis of Leibnitz, which seemed so scandalous to Arnauld: "The notion of each individual includes *a priori* all the events that will happen to him." According to this dialectical fatalism, the fact that Alexander the Great would die in Babylon is a quality of that king, like arrogance.

rapidity with which he could utter fatal words." [2] He gave the century what the century demanded—*comédies larmoyantes* for the many and verbal arabesques for the few—and he executed those dissimilar things with a kind of negligent glee. His perfection has been a disadvantage; his work is so harmonious that it may seem inevitable and even trite. It is hard for us to imagine the universe without Wilde's epigrams; but that difficulty does not make them less plausible.

An aside: Oscar Wilde's name is linked to the cities of the plain; his fame, to condemnation and jail. Nevertheless (this has been perceived very clearly by Hesketh Pearson) the fundamental spirit of his work is joy. On the other hand, the powerful work of Chesterton, the prototype of physical and moral sanity, is always on the verge of becoming a nightmare. The diabolical and the horrible lie in wait on his pages; the most innocuous subject can assume the forms of terror. Chesterton is a man who wants to regain childhood; Wilde, a man who keeps an invulnerable innocence in spite of the habits of evil and misfortune.

Like Chesterton, like Lang, like Boswell, Wilde is among those fortunate writers who can do without the approval of the critics and even, at times, without the reader's approval, and the pleasure we derive from his company is irresistible and constant.

[2] This sentence is by Reyes, who applies it to the Mexican male (*Reloj de sol,* p. 158).

Oscar Wilde

by Brendan Behan

For Sean O'Sullivan

*Oscar Wilde, Poète et Dramaturge,
né à Dublin le 15 Octobre, 1856,
est mort dans cette maison
le 30 Novembre, 1900.*

After all the strife,
That, alive, he caused,
Ravaged with fear,
In the half-light stretched,
The gay spark's body
Lies dumb in the dark,
Silent, the funereal
Candles guttering.
The graceful body,
The firm gaze, spent
In a cold bare room
With a concierge spiteful
From too much attendance
On a foreign tippler
Who left without paying
The ten per cent service.
Exiled from the Flore
To a saintly desert,

The young prince of sin
A withered churl,
The gold jewel of lust
Left far behind him,
No Pernod to brace him
Only holy water,
The young king of Beauty
A ravished Narcissus
As the star of the pure Virgin
Glows on the water

Envoi

Delightful the path of sin
But a holy death's a habit.
Good man yourself there, Oscar,
Every way you had it.

Chronology of Important Dates

1854	Birth of Wilde in Dublin, October 16.
1871–74	Attended Trinity College, Dublin.
1874	Matriculated at Magdalen College, Oxford.
1878	Took first-class in Classical Moderations and Litterae Humaniores, and won the Newdigate prize for poetry.
1881	Publication of *Poems*. Lecture tour of the United States, December 24, 1881 to December 27, 1882.
1884	Married Constance Lloyd, May 29.
1887–89	Edited *The Woman's World*.
1891	Publication of *The Soul of Man under Socialism, The Picture of Dorian Gray, Intentions, Lord Arthur Savile's Crime and Other Stories,* and *A House of Pomegranates*. Met Lord Alfred Douglas.
1892	First performance of *Lady Windermere's Fan*, February 20.
1893	Publication of *Salome*. Performance of *A Woman of No Importance*.
1895	First performance of *An Ideal Husband*, January 3, and of *The Importance of Being Earnest*, February 14. Trial, and acquittal, of Douglas' father, the Marquis of Queensberry, on charges of having libeled Wilde, April 3–5. Wilde's two trials on charges of homosexuality, the first resulting in a hung jury, the second in conviction, April 26 to May 1, and May 20–25.
1897	Wrote *De Profundis* letter to Douglas, March. Released from prison, May 19. Went to live on the continent.
1898	Publication of *The Ballad of Reading Gaol*.
1900	Death of Wilde in Paris, November 30.

Notes on the Editor and Contributors

RICHARD ELLMANN, editor of this volume, now at Yale, will be Goldsmiths' Professor of English Literature at Oxford from 1970. He won the National Book Award in 1959 for his biography of James Joyce.

W. H. AUDEN, the famous poet, was born in England and now lives in the United States.

BRENDAN BEHAN (1923–1964), the Irish dramatist and poet, wrote among other books *Borstal Boy* and *The Quare Fellow*.

ERIC BENTLEY has been Brander Matthews Professor of Dramatic Literature at Columbia University, and is the author of books on Shaw, Brecht, and the modern theatre.

JOHN BETJEMAN, English poet.

JORGE LUIS BORGES (b. 1899) is the Argentinian poet, fiction writer, and critic, who has recently held the Charles Eliot Norton Professorship at Harvard.

HART CRANE (1899–1932), American poet.

LORD ALFRED DOUGLAS (1870–1945), English poet, known chiefly for his friendship with Wilde.

ANDRÉ GIDE (1869–1951), the French novelist and critic.

ST. JOHN HANKIN (1869–1909), English dramatist and critic.

LIONEL JOHNSON (1867–1901), English poet and critic.

JAMES JOYCE (1882–1941), the Irish novelist.

G. WILSON KNIGHT, English critic, author of books on Shakespeare, Byron, and others.

THOMAS MANN (1875–1955), the German novelist.

MARY MCCARTHY, American novelist and critic.

WALTER PATER (1839–1894), English historian of art and literary critic.

EDOUARD RODITI, American critic and poet.

GEORGE WOODCOCK, Canadian-born critic and poet.

W. B. YEATS (1865–1939), the Irish poet.

Selected Bibliography

No authoritative edition of all Wilde's writings exists, though the many available collections are fairly accurate if incomplete. Wilde's *Letters* have been excellently edited by Rupert Hart-Davis (London, 1962). His principal writings about literature and society are included in *The Artist as Critic: Critical Writings of Oscar Wilde*, ed. Richard Ellmann (New York, 1969). The first life was by Robert Sherard (*The Life of Oscar Wilde*, New York, 1906), on the foundation of which Frank Harris embroidered his own recollections in *Oscar Wilde, His Life and Confessions* (Garden City, New York, 1930). Hesketh Pearson, *The Life of Oscar Wilde* (London, 1954) has collected most of the anecdotes about Wilde. H. Montgomery Hyde, *Oscar Wilde: The Aftermath* (New York, 1963), discloses much new information about Wilde's prison experiences and his activities following his release. A lively account of Wilde's American lecture tour is in Lloyd Lewis and Henry Justin Smith, *Oscar Wilde Discovers America* (New York, 1936). H. Montgomery Hyde has also edited *Oscar Wilde* in the Famous Trials Series (Penguin, 1962). The effect of disgrace upon Wilde's family is the subject of Vyvyan Holland, *Son of Oscar Wilde* (New York, 1954). Lord Alfred Douglas wrote several books of reminiscence in which Wilde figures prominently, but a more consistent picture of that relationship appears in Rupert Croft-Cooke, *Bosie* (New York, 1963). The most recent life is Philippe Jullian, *Oscar Wilde* (Paris, 1967).

Among other useful books may be mentioned Robert Merle, *Oscar Wilde ou la "destinée" de l'homosexuel* (Paris, 1955); Vincent O'Sullivan, *Aspects of Wilde* (London, 1938); Edouard Roditi, *Oscar Wilde* (Norfolk, Connecticut, 1947); Susan Sontag, *Against Interpretation* (New York, 1966), and Epifanio San Juan, Jr., *The Art of Oscar Wilde* (Princeton, 1967).

TWENTIETH CENTURY VIEWS

British Authors